Winthrop Mackworth Praed, George Young

The political and occasional Poems of Winthrop Mackworth Praed

Winthrop Mackworth Praed, George Young

The political and occasional Poems of Winthrop Mackworth Praed

ISBN/EAN: 9783337133146

Printed in Europe, USA, Canada, Australia, Japan

Cover: Foto ©ninafisch / pixelio.de

More available books at **www.hansebooks.com**

THE

Political and Occasional Poems

OF

WINTHROP MACKWORTH PRAED

EDITED, WITH NOTES, BY

SIR GEORGE YOUNG

WARD, LOCK, AND CO
LONDON: WARWICK HOUSE, SALISBURY SQUARE, E.C.
NEW YORK: BOND STREET.
1888.

CONTENTS.

PART I. 1823—1830.

                                                        PAGE

I. A FREE TRANSLATION OF A LETTER FROM PRINCE HILT TO A FRIEND AT PARIS 3
II. CHANCERY MORALS 7
III. LETTERS TO ILLUSTRIOUS CHARACTERS :—
    I.—A Complimentary Epistle to the Emperor of Russia 11
IV. LETTERS TO ILLUSTRIOUS CHARACTERS :—
    II.—To la Desirée of le Desiré 15
V. LOVE'S ETERNITY 19
VI. A SONG OF IMPOSSIBILITIES 23
VII. ODE TO THE CHANCELLOR 28
VIII. WISDOM OF THE GREAT COUNCIL. I. . . . 31
IX. WISDOM OF THE GREAT COUNCIL. II. . . . 36
X. THE LAY OF THE CHEESE 41
XI. ROYAL EDUCATION 45
XII. THE CORONATION OF CHARLES X. :—
    I.—The Journey to Rheims 49

CONTENTS.

	PAGE
XIII. THE CORONATION OF CHARLES X. :—	
II.—Rheims	54
XIV. THE LONDON UNIVERSITY	61
XV. AN EPITAPH ON THE LATE KING OF THE SANDWICH ISLANDS	66
XVI. THE CHAUNTS OF THE BRAZEN HEAD. I.	72
XVII. THE CHAUNTS OF THE BRAZEN HEAD. II.	78
XVIII. THE CHAUNTS OF THE BRAZEN HEAD. III.	81
XIX. UTOPIA	84
XX. THE DEATH OF CANNING	90
XXI. THE RIDDLES OF THE SPHINX	93
XXII. THE OUTS	97
XXIII. THE RETROSPECT	100
XXIV. BIGOTRY'S REMONSTRANCE	103
XXV. TWENTY-EIGHT AND TWENTY-NINE	107
XXVI. WATERLOO	113
XXVII. MARS DISARMED BY LOVE	117

PART II. 1830—1834.

I. THE NEW ORDER OF THINGS	123
II. THE CONVERT	126
III. ODE TO POPULARITY	129
IV. THE COMPLAINT OF LIBERTY	133
V. WHY AND WHEREFORE	137
VI. KING ALFRED'S BOOK	140
VII. INTENTIONS	144
VIII. THE BEGGAR'S PETITION	148
IX. SPEECH OF THE IRISH SECRETARY IN DEFENCE OF THE LORD LIEUTENANT	151

CONTENTS.

		PAGE
X.	SPEECH DELIVERED BY A WORTHY ALDERMAN, SEVERAL TIMES, IN COMMITTEE ON THE REFORM BILL	155
XI.	THE BILL, THE WHOLE BILL, AND NOTHING BUT THE BILL	159
XII.	REASONS FOR NOT RATTING	163
XIII.	THE OLD TORY	165
XIV.	THE YOUNG WHIG	168
XV.	ODE ADDRESSED TO THE RT. HON. POULETT THOMSON, ON HIS DISCOVERY OF THE FRUCTIFYING PRINCIPLE	171
XVI.	THE DREAM OF A REPORTER	175
XVII.	THE NEW LIGHT	179
XVIII.	LONG AGO	183
XIX.	PLUS DE POLITIQUE	185
XX.	THE MAGIC BENCH	188
XXI.	PLEDGES	192
XXII.	HUME TRANSLATED	195
XXIII.	THE OLD SOLDIER	198
XXIV.	A CABINET CAROL	201
XXV.	STANZAS BY A TEN-POUNDER OBJECTED TO	204
XXVI.	AN EPISTLE FROM AN OLD ELECTIONEERER	207
XXVII.	THE BEGGAR'S THANKS	210
XXVIII.	A NURSERY SONG	212
XXIX.	STANZAS ON SEEING THE SPEAKER ASLEEP	214
XXX.	PATRIOT AND PLACEMAN	217
XXXI.	WHISTLE	220
XXXII.	THE ADIEUS OF WESTMINSTER	223
XXXIII.	THIRTY-TWO AND THIRTY-THREE	228
XXXIV.	THE WASHING OF THE BLACKAMOOR	231
XXXV.	MR LITTLETON'S FRIENDSHIP	235

		PAGE
XXXVI.	THE REMONSTRANCE	238
XXXVII.	THE RUSSELL MELODIES.—I.	241
XXXVIII.	THE RUSSELL MELODIES.—II.	244
XXXIX.	THE RUSSELL MELODIES.—III.	248
XL.	THE RUSSELL MELODIES.—IV.	251
XLI.	THE RUSSELL MELODIES.—V.	254
XLII.	THE RUSSELL MELODIES.—VI.	256
XLIII.	MAXIMS	259
XLIV.	THE SONG OF THE NURSE	262
XLV.	THE STATE OF THE NATION	266
XLVI.	A MEMBER'S MUSINGS	269
XLVII.	COUNSELS OF A FATHER TO HIS SON	271
XLVIII.	THE WHISPERS OF THE RUE RIVOLI	274
XLIX.	THE FALSE REPORT	277
L.	A FAMILIAR EPISTLE	279
LI.	COLLOQUIES OF THE CANONGATE	282
LII.	THE LATE RESIGNATIONS	285
LIII.	THE SONG OF THE BELLS	288
LIV.	LINES WRITTEN UNDER A PORTRAIT OF LORD MAYO, DRAWN BY THE QUEEN	290

PART III. 1859.

I.	THE CONTESTED ELECTION	293
II.	THE POLITICAL DRAWING-ROOM	307
III.	THE TREASURY BENCH	313

INTRODUCTION.

The Political Poems of Winthrop Mackworth Praed are here offered to the public in a collected form ; and an engagement undertaken many years ago, when these pieces were omitted from the edition of his Poems in two volumes which was published in 1864, with my assistance, by the late Rev. Derwent Coleridge, is thus fulfilled. In the interval I have been enabled to make the list more complete than it could at that time have been made, particularly in respect of the poems here included in Part I. of the volume ; and the lapse of time has removed some objections, resting upon personal considerations, to the republication of the whole. The necessary information for selecting poems of Praed's authorship from among a multitude of others, scattered through the columns of a variety of newspapers, has been derived in the first place from manuscripts and scrap-books in the possession of members of the poet's family, and from the recollections, above all, of the sister who was, during the whole period covered by the first and second series, his principal correspondent, and the depositary of his confidence. In the second place, I have learnt important items in conversation with contemporaries of the author, since deceased, especially from Lord Macaulay, Lord Belper, and Mr. Charles Knight. For the second series the principal authority is a little volume privately printed for the author in 1835, containing forty-seven pieces. This reprint affords no additional notes and very few corrections, and appears to have been produced almost without supervision, probably from a newspaper scrap-book. The Third Part consists of three satires (one unfinished) which were found among the poet's papers after his death, fairly copied for the press, for which he probably intended them. With the exception of a quotation in Sir George Trevelyan's *Life of Macaulay*, and the concluding lines, "God save the Queen," no part of these has ever before been printed; and they will, no doubt, be welcome to many, as exhibiting in its maturity the consummate art of Praed's peculiar style. On the strength of these later poems it appears probable that a high place might have been claimed by their author had he lived—perhaps may yet be claimed for him—among Satirists.

In deciding what pieces to include in this collection, I have taken as a test the prevalence of allusions to persons then living, and to measures then under consideration. Three pieces in this volume have appeared before, in the collected edition of *Praed's Poems*, and eight others in the Selection which I edited for *Moxon's Miniature Poets*. The rest are either collected from the periodicals in which they appeared, reprinted from the privately printed edition of 1835, or now first published from MSS. in the possession of the poet's family.

"The Devil's Decoy," misnamed by the publisher "The Red Fisherman," might, strictly speaking, have been added to this volume; for it was, according to Charles Knight, a personal and political pasquinade, written in scorn of the attitude taken up by churchmen, by Dr. Henry Philpotts especially, in the last stage of the controversy upon the Catholic claims. But its picturesque scenery and sparkling versification have long ago vindicated for it a place among poems which are not dependent, for appreciation, upon an explanation of forgotten allusions; and the moral of it is sufficiently free from occasional matter to enable it to stand alone. An inquiry once appeared in *Notes and Queries*, what was the source laid under contribution by Praed for the legend of the poem. I know of none; and I believe the whole to have been, in the fullest sense, the creation of his fancy.

There are still in existence a few copies of a pamphlet entitled *Trash*, in which the squibs of the St. Ives' election of 1832, unsuccessfully conducted by Praed on the Conservative side against Mr. James Halse as a Reformer, were reprinted for the benefit of those interested in the borough, or in the fortunes of the defeated candidate. They were naturally of a slight and local character, not intended for preservation, and have been omitted in accordance with what, it is believed, would have been the decided opinion of the writer himself.

The dates, sources and circumstances of these pieces, and explanations of the forgotten allusions, have been set forth in notes prefixed to each poem. Some illustrative passages have been added from the poet's correspondence with the member of his family above mentioned, and from other sources. The notices of contemporary politics, which appeared to be required for a full appreciation of the satire conveyed, have been made as short as possible. For want of a little editorial work of this kind the pasquinades of Moore have been left on the shelf in an unreadable condition.

Something may properly be here said in reference to the change of party, exhibited in the second and third series included in this volume, as compared with the first. That at Cambridge as an undergraduate, and afterwards in London, as a young man of twenty-three, Praed was, or believed himself to be, a "Radical Reformer;" that he was associated, as such, with Charles Austin, Macaulay, Edward Strutt (afterwards Lord Belper), and others, who afterwards were known as Whigs; and that many at the time considered his entrance into public life as a follower of Peel to be an apostasy from his previous Liberalism—so much is undeniable. But it is fair to remark, that whatever might have been said of those who, between 1827 and 1832, changed from Toryism to Liberalism, the man whose change was in the opposite direction could have had little beside honest conviction to influence him. That apart from insincerity and interested motive there is anything wrong in itself or requiring defence on moral grounds in a young man of twenty-eight entering public life on the side opposite to that to which till five years before he had been ardently attached, will hardly be maintained. From the time when Praed became a public man his consistency was unimpeachable. This is more than can be said of some who assailed him, on this pretext, in public life. For instance, Bulwer Lytton, the ringleader in a concerted attack upon him, which was made in the House of Commons, on the ground of his change of politics, in the year before his death, was opposed to the Catholic claims at college, became a Radical when he entered Parliament, and some years later was again a Conservative, and died an honoured pillar of that party. It is evident from the satire on himself which he embodied in his parody of a Union Debate at Cambridge, that Praed was not in his undergraduate days a Reformer of a very reasoning type. Although born of a Whig family, and although brought up amidst traditions of admiration for Milton and Cowper, the favourite poets of the Whig household at the time, his own cast of mind, even from early days, led him into the camp of the Romantic Revival; and of his Radical "sturm und drang" but little survived to him save a decided objection to religious intolerance. To such a temperament the advent of Canning to the first place in the State, his sympathy with constitutional liberty abroad, and with Catholic Emancipation at home, appealed with irresistible force: and had Canning lived it may safely be concluded that Praed would have found himself at home in the following of one with whom he had so much, besides their common Etonian celebrity, in common. But Canning died, and all that Praed could do he did, to record his admiration and regret (See Part I., No. XX.) It is noticeable that of Canning's enemies Lord Grey rather than Peel is the subject of his animosity on this occasion. Lord Lansdowne, who had supported Canning, received (Part I., No. XXIV.) the last tribute of allegiance which he paid to a Liberal leader. When the ranks of the two parties closed up for the great struggle of the Reform Bill he found himself, without any conscious dereliction of his previously formed opinions, more in harmony with Peel than with Brougham. The passing of the Catholic Emancipation Act had removed the barrier between himself and the new Conservative Party which Peel was forming, after Eldon's exit, and after Wellington's failure. Thus, though the remnant of Canning's official circle —Palmerston, Goderich, Grant and Lamb—found it comparatively easy to join the Whigs and to swim with the tide of Liberalism, Praed gravitated, almost alone, towards Conservatism, and took up deliberately with the falling cause of the existing Ministry, in the hope that after a time it would return to power, but without much solicitude for present advancement.

His position and his views are pretty clearly worked out in the extracts from private letters which follow; letters written to his sister, the present editor's mother.

"10*th February*, 1830.—The entrance of my friend Macaulay into the great council of the nation gives me, as you will suppose, the greatest pleasure. I cannot but think that he must be the greatest man there by-and-by, and I have bespoken his first frank, in the expectation of selling it for ten pounds thirty years hence.

"17*th February*.—What I am going to say next is very strictly confidential ; it was only to be confined to myself, but you are myself. Do you know that it is scarcely impossible that a seat in parliament for a Government borough may be offered me before the end of this session ? Fitzgerald, through whom all overtures of this kind come to me, has been consulted as to my probable sentiments by his cousin ; and has been examined at great length by Peel, touching the same matter. The upshot of the affair is, that the ministers are a little alarmed at Macaulay's intrusion ; and that Peel finds himself, by Vesey's retreat, left absolutely alone, so far as speaking is concerned, on that side of the House. The first question put to my friend was, ' Whether my intimacy with Macaulay was very close ?' and the next, ' Whether I should, in consequence of it, be unwilling to be pitted against him ' (Peel's words) 'in the House ?' To both these questions Fitzgerald answered as I should have done, that my friendship with Macaulay was the closest possible : and that I should certainly refuse to occupy any post in which I should be expected to place myself in personal collision with any man. Then, as to my general principles and opinions, he said he had not observed anything in them which should prevent me from giving generally my support to the present Administration ; and finally assured his great man that I should never take any undue advantage of such communications as might be made me. Ultimately it is settled that Vesey, before he leaves this country, is to make me known to Peel ; and for the rest—what do you think ? for I only heard all this last night, and have not yet thought at all about it."

His decision, naturally enough, was to accept the proposal if made ; and the matter progressed so far that a seat for the borough of Wenlock was named, though not to himself, as destined for him. But nothing, at this time, came of it; and by the 2nd March, when Macaulay made his debut in the House of Commons, the matter was understood to be at an end, his introductions to the chiefs of the party having got no farther than Mr. Herries. Nevertheless, from this time he had chosen his side, and in December of the same year he was enabled to purchase a seat for the remaining two years (as was anticipated) of that Parliament, and entered the House accordingly, (but on the opposition side, the Tories having in the meantime resigned office,) as one of the members for the borough of St. Germains. He writes to the same correspondent :—

"5th December, 1830.—I am very anxious that you should not think me *non compos* for this step I take, and therefore I will try to state my view of the case. I pay £1,000 for a seat for two years. Now, I will first consider the certain results if I fail in the house, and afterwards the probable and possible results if I succeed there.

*   *   *   *   *   *

"All this would not be satisfactory if I were convinced that I was sacrificing my integrity to what would be at best a doubtful hope of advancement in the world. Therefore I certainly consulted my own feelings as scrupulously as I could. I never could have supported a party opposed to Catholic Emancipation. That question is gone. We shall have to think about reform, retrenchment, the bank charter, the East India Company's charter, the West India question. On the three last I agree with the Outs far more decidedly than with the Ins. As to retrenchment, I do not think much more can be done than the Duke was willing to do. But if the Whigs contrive it, they will scarcely be opposed. For reform, my opinions at college were certainly pretty strong in favour of it; but they were never in favour of such a reform as it is likely the Whigs will introduce. We shall see. It is not unlikely, I think, *entre nous*, that the Out party may suffer it to pass quietly. Upon their return, if ever they return, to place, it would be well to have it out of their way."

Once in Parliament his career was brilliant. In the early debates on the Reform Bill of 1831 he avoided the encounter with Macaulay, which was undertaken by Croker with some temporary success; and his principal effort was a speech on a financial subject. When the Bill was in Committee he took an active part, as a party man, in the discussions; and two speeches of his, on moving amendments, the one, that in counties to which three members were assigned each constituent should have the right of voting for two candidates only, and the other, that freeholds within the limits of boroughs should confer votes for the borough, and not for the county, received much approval, and were reprinted as pamphlets. The selection of these points seems to show, in the light of the subsequent history of the question, that he was possessed of considerable political sagacity. Of the former of the two, the same provision that was afterwards embodied by Disraeli in the Reform Bill of 1867, and superseded in 1886 by the one member constituencies, he writes:—

"18*th August*, 1831.—On Saturday last I moved a very

important amendment—important in my own eyes, but so novel in its nature that I could not get Peel or any of our leaders except Herries to listen to it for a moment. I brought it forward on a day on which it was arranged that no discussion should take place, and on which, consequently, the House was very thinly attended. I had taken great pains with the arrangement of my argument, and I have reason to think I was very successful in its exposition. Lord Althorp replied at considerable length, opposing my view, but giving me credit for great ingenuity. Since the discussion many men, some of whose names I have not yet learnt, have applied to me in the House for explanation on particular points of my statement, and the proposal, novel as it is, seems to have met with so much favour, that I am thinking of trying a division upon it in a future stage of the Bill.

"30*th September*, 1831.—I have to thank you for ... the Admiral's (Ekins) disquisition. He is perfectly right as to the extent to which my principle would be carried by absolute truth. But the fact is, that the original fault lies higher up in the system. It is wrong to give more than one representative to any one constituency. Of course the effect of his proposal in the case which I have argued would be to send three men to Parliament by three different sets of votes. The better plan would be to divide your one big constituency into three small ones. See the short observation in my speech on the division of counties, and the manner in which that step will forward the attainment of fair representation. ... But people will consider nothing which does not seem calculated to serve one or other of our conflicting parties."

The Session of 1832 opened favourably for Praed. A very successful speech on his second amendment, above noticed, effaced the memory of a comparative failure of his in the debate on the second reading of the second Bill, made during the autumn of the year before. Sir Robert Peel, the last of the statesmen, in the political history of our time, who had the wit to form about him a school of his younger followers, soon became very friendly with him. On the 6th February he writes :—

"I continue to receive felicitations on all sides. But what a lottery is Parliamentary fame! The subject on which I spoke the other evening had undoubtedly occupied much of my thoughts; but expecting that Mr. Goulburn would have opened the question, and that my part would have been to take off the objections of some of our opponents, I had bestowed even less study than usual on the arrangement of my arguments or the structure of my sentences. And nothing that I have before done has earned me half the praise of this. . . . I was pleased to be told yesterday, by one of our friends, that Sir R. Peel speaks of *liking* me better (without reference to his estimate of my abilities) than any other of his young recruits. I was pleased, partly because I respect and admire Sir Robert very much, and am therefore glad to stand well in his good graces, and partly because my vanity is flattered by a confirmation of an opinion which I had previously formed. For I think I have told you before that I fancied there was more of friendliness and cordiality in his manner to me than he is said to use towards all men. I do not forget his advice to me to 'go home and get to bed,' when others whom the world would call kinder were complimenting me on what did not deserve compliments."

On the passing of the Bill St. Germains was disfranchised, and Praed's candidature at the general election for the borough of St. Ives, where he had some family interest, proved unsuccessful. He remained out of Parliament till 1835. In the interval, from August 1832 to August 1834, he wrote regularly in the *Morning Post*, and by his efforts raised it to the leading position among Conservative papers. The later and larger half of the pieces contained in Part II. of this volume were so written. The following are extracts from letters of this period:—

"*5th April*, 1833.—The reports which my friends give me of the present state of the House of Commons are not such as to inspire me with any very strong wish to be just now a member of it; it seems to be a more ignorant and less reasonable assembly than it ever was before. The speakers are far more numerous than they were, and everybody admits that the speeches are far more dull.

"26th *May*, 1833.—Many of the prose papers I have done have been much noticed, and I believe the paper benefits by my services, which, however, I hope after one more year my professional advancement will force me to discontinue.

"29th *June*, 1833.—My most gratifying dinner, considered with reference to my vanity, was my 'old fish dinner.' Long ago, in the time of Mr. Pitt, it became the custom for the cabinet ministers, and a very few others whom they associated by ballot, to go down to Greenwich once in the summer and dine upon fish. This sort of club kept up its annual voyage till 1831, when for the first time, the Tories being out of office, the dinner was not eaten. Last year it was talked of, but not revived. This year the laudable custom was re-established, and among the new people to be invited the Duke of Wellington put my name down almost the first.

"15th *July*, 1833.—John Murray requested me the other day to draw my pen in the service of the *Quarterly*, being induced to do so by hearing that I was reputed the author of a very pointed paper in the *Morning Post*, which had been noticed to him by Mr. Hallam, the author of various works. Mr. Hallam, you know, is a Whig."

On October 15th, 1833, he was staying with the Duke of Wellington at Walmer Castle; and on January 6th, 1834, he writes:—

"Contrary to my usual practice, I came from Cambridge to town, being moved thereto by a letter from the Duke, in which he begged me to do with my own hand his defence against a certain attack of the *Times*. The defence, hurriedly executed, is in to-day's *Post*. *Apropos* of the *Post*, I had no hand in "1833 and 1834," whatever it may be. I have not yet seen it. My papers about the changes in the Ordnance Department, done from Sir H. Hardinge's and the Duke's hints, made much noise, and contributed to the overthrow of the scheme, which is abandoned."

The dismissal of the Whig Ministry in November 1834 made it evident that another general election was impending; and Praed accepted the candidature, in the Conservative interest, for Great Yarmouth.

While canvassing, he was offered by Peel, and accepted, the Secretaryship to the Board of Control, which he held accordingly during the short-lived Conservative Administration of 1835. To this period belong the following extracts:—

"16*th December*, 1834.—Since I wrote my letter I went canvassing with young Lacon, returned to Ormesby at twelve, found a breathless messenger waiting to hurry me back to Yarmouth, where a despatch awaited me from Sir R. Peel. I hastened to Yarmouth, found a huge packet, sent by the guard of the mail, there being no post (Monday). I found it contained, as you may suppose, an offer of office, the Secretaryship of the Board of Control. Accept. or not? As to my *interest*, it was a difficult question. As to my duty, I thought it a plain one; I accepted or determined to accept. I called my principal supporters together; consulted them; was assured my prospects would be benefited rather than injured by the change in my position; started by the mail that night; saw Peel this morning; visited Lord Ellenborough at *our* office, and, in short, became a great man, for—how long a time? No matter; I am *right*. Peel has difficulties enough to contend with; why add a molehill to his mountain?

"7*th February*, 1835, Board of Control.—We shall soon be in the thick of the fight now, wherein all our friends predict that we shall win glorious victories; and wherein I prognosticate, as is my wont, disastrous defeats. However, whatever out-turn this speculation may give us, it will be something to have been a supporter and, in a small way, a member of the last Government which will deserve the name of a Government in Great Britain. Brutus in Lucan goes to consult Cato on the propriety of engaging in the Civil War. Cato deprecates Civil War in general. But, quoth he, in some very fine verses, ' Far from me be the reproach that I folded my arms in sloth while that empire was falling, by whose fall the farthest ends of the world will be moved.' So say I: and amid the overthrow it will be a consolation that I was thought fit to hold a commission!

"*A propos* of commissions, what think you of the commission on the affair of the Church? It is to me all I ever wanted, all I ever preached. Most unfortunate shall we be if a scheme so wise and so honest for the advancement of sound religion shall be overthrown by the mere operation of party spirit and factious animosity. What a tale it will be for history to tell if Church Reform, thus boldly and yet temperately commenced, shall be taken from the hands of the archbishops and bishops of the Church to be handed over to the Humes and O'Connells who are so ready to begin upon the task!

"But I see no reflection or reason among men; it is all 'Turn out the Tories!' on one side; and it is all 'Keep out the Whigs!' on the other. Another fortnight will enable us to see more clearly what is to become of us.

"13th March, 1835.—The ministry appears to gather strength. Their victory on the repeal of the Malt Tax was a very decisive one. But so many of their supporters, members for agricultural constituencies, have disappointed their constituents by their vote, that I imagine it will be impossible for Sir R. Peel to dissolve parliament with any chance of *bettering himself*, whatever excesses his opponents may commit. We are, therefore, in a situation of no small difficulty still. The enemy, however, if we may judge by Hume's withdrawal of his motion for limiting the supplies, do not feel their post one of absolute confidence.

"There have been two or three conversations in the House upon matters of business connected with East India affairs, in which I have had to take part. These occasions of *necessary* appearance in debate are very advantageous to a young member.

"31st March, 1835.—The debate of last night was the opening of the grand attack upon us. Read Sir J. Graham's speech, particularly the close of it. It is all noble; not only intellectually powerful, but morally sublime. It is of no use, however; we shall be beat by thirty or forty. I expect that Sir R. Peel will then retire. We shall see. But my anticipations are as gloomy as ever; and I find none to sympathize with me.

"With respect to Church Property: Tithe has always been a less valuable property than rent—from the difference of the laws by which its collection is authorized, and other causes. A man could always buy £100 a year in *tithe* for the price he would pay for £80 a year in *rent*. Now, our Bill proposes to give to tithe the nature of rent. Of course, therefore, you do not change the value of a certain tithe, if giving to it the qualities of rent you reduce it to the value which as rent it would bear. A man has £100 a year—or the Church, if you will, has £100 a year—in tithe. We say we will give you *rent* for tithe; but not £100 of rent for £100 of tithe; no, £80 of rent for £100 of tithe. Deducting £5 for the fees of collection, you have the £75 our Bill proposes. And there is not much 'robbery' in it, *comprenez-vous*?

"*4th April*, 1835.—In another week I reckon upon having more leisure. The progress of events will roll me out of the India Board in a few days.

"If you have been studying the debates of the past week, I think nothing I can say will add to your amazement at the length to which party spirit will hurry men. Truth and reason and policy all seem to be one way, and numbers are uniformly the other.

"My course is one which I by no means repent of; and if it were yet to be chosen I would not make a different choice. I am, therefore, personally, very indifferent as to the result. You know, I have never been sanguine enough to be now much disappointed; and if my ambition as a politician is nipped my vanity as a conjurer grows.

"*6th April*, 1835.—I have not read any of the reports of my speech; but from your remark about the inexpediency of teaching to read on an empty stomach, I think my argument thereanent must have been imperfectly (though not incorrectly) stated. My argument was: (1) That as the right of property in the alleged alienable £200,000 was denied by our opponents, they must make out the expediency of levying that sum for a particular purpose by way of tax. (2) That from so distressed a population as that of Ireland the levying of such a sum for the purpose of education was a monstrous absurdity. (3) That the same sum in the hands of humane and pious men, though of the Protestant faith, as at present, would be much more usefully employed, part of it actually going for purposes of education, and part in the relief of those physical sufferings for which the Instruction Tax would of course do nothing. The same argument was used with more force by Lord Stanley; and the circumstance is gratifying to my vanity, whether I had happened to anticipate his reasoning or he to imitate mine. You do not like Lord Stanley's speech well enough .... He has raised himself in my judgment by his speech; though I think his present policy abominable. His refusal to join Sir R. Peel, to which our present difficulties are mainly attributable, is said to be dictated by a personal hostility to the Duke. You may imagine that *I* have little toleration for such a sentiment.

"I continue to anticipate a change of Government in the course of this week. Lord Ellenborough tells me he thinks *no Radicals* will come in. If he is correct, I have no notion how a Government is to be formed. We can only expect a miserable piece of patchwork, which will go to pieces of itself in another month. Ultimately we *must* have O'Connell and his gang.

"*9th April*, 1835.—I wrote you a hurried line yesterday to say that we were all out; or at least, only holding office till the appointment of our successors. To-day I write to tell you what I trust it is hardly necessary to tell, that whether from philosophy or indifference, or something better than either, I am very little moved by the change, and acquiesce with perfect tranquillity in my altered fortune.

"We know nothing yet of the progress of the new arrangements. The expectation is that Lord Grey will be—some say, has been—sent for by the king. I think, however, it is, as yet, mere opinion. People imagine, that if he should be summoned, he would endeavour to construct a patchwork Government—a few Whigs, a few Tories, a few no-party men; at all events, it is gossipped that he will have no Radicals. I think otherwise of Lord Grey; he came into office before, full of protestations about safe and moderate Reform; and he proceeded to introduce the 'Whole Bill.' He came in loud in vows of his allegiance to his 'Order;' and soon recommended the destruction of it by the creation of one hundred peers. If he comes in again now he will make professions with equal ostentation, and break them with equal facility. He cannot, in fact, do otherwise. He has made the House of Commons such that there is no room in it for moderate men. Radicalism is in the ascendant, and no Government can go on without the O'Connells.

To tell how Government did " go on without the O'Connells," and how, for that purpose, the great central mass of outsiders in politics found it necessary for a time to sink their Liberalism, until the Free Trade question revived it, is beyond the date of Praed's career, and consequently beyond the purpose of these notes. His work in the House of Commons during the three years that remained to him was not conspicuous, but was generally creditable; a protest, in his character as an ex-official, against saddling the revenues of India with the burden of a job for the benefit of the Bombay Marine, a speech against the abominable insincerity of Election Committees, and a vote on the same occasion for a resolution of O'Connell's, in the opposite lobby to that in which the leaders of both parties found themselves, were his most memorable acts. In company with Derwent Coleridge, his biographer, he worked hard at the foundation of the National Society, which has organized, for churchmen, the Elementary Schools in England. In the summer of 1838 his health began to fail, and he died of a rapid consumption in July 1839.

The present appears a suitable occasion to set at rest certain doubts as to the authorship of poems, which were by Praed's last American editor, Mr. W. H. Whitmore, erroneously ascribed to his pen, and were excluded by Derwent Coleridge from the collected edition. The error has recently been repeated, with less excuse, by a London publisher. The difficulty, such as it is, arises out of the common use, at the same time and in the same periodicals, of one and the same initial by way of signature, the Greek uncial Φ, by Praed, and by his friend Edward M. Fitzgerald. This Fitzgerald is by no means to be confounded with the "hoarse Fitzgerald" of Byron's *English Bards and Scotch Reviewers*, who was parodied in the first piece of the *Rejected Addresses;* and still less with the Edward Fitzgerald who rewrote *Omar Khayam* and the *Agamemnon* of Æschylus in English. He was a cousin of Mr. Vesey Fitzgerald, whose defeat for the County Clare in 1828 converted the Duke of Wellington to Catholic Emancipation; he was an Irishman, possessed of some talent for verse, and some social gifts, and he died some years after Praed's death, which happened in 1839. Two or three poems of his, written in imitation of Praed, have been included by Mr. Locker Lampson in his

Lyra Elegantiarum; he has also left some good political pieces; but apart from Praed's inspiration, I do not think there is anything of his composing which merits notice, unless it be a bitter lampoon on Thomas Moore, which appeared in the *Morning Post* of 25th September, 1835. In distinguishing his pieces from Praed's it has been impossible for me to ignore in him a certain ingrained vulgarity, a deficiency of accurate knowledge of Latin, an imperfect mastery of metre, an indifference to grammar, and a laxity in rhyming, which, together with a fondness for musical slang, for Irish allusions, and for quotations from Byron, make up the notes of a rather unsatisfactory writer. How different from these are the characteristics of Praed's style his admirers will not need to be informed; and it is nothing less than a duty in his editor to protect Praed's memory from the ascription of pieces impossible for him to have written and quite unworthy of his fame.

The signature Φ first appears in the *New Monthly Magazine* in the years 1821-4.* The pieces so signed are spiritless and sentimental; and when compared with Praed's contemporaneous poetry in Knights' *Quarterly Magazine*, will not be attributed to him. Meantime, in the *Morning Chronicle* of 1823-5 there appeared over the same signature the majority of the poems contained in Part I. of this volume, a sufficient number of which are known to be Praed's to justify the ascription of the whole series to him. Praed retained the same initial for two of his known contributions to the *Sphynx* in 1827, and for one of those which he sent to *Friendship's Offering* for 1828. So far no doubt or difficulty arises. That Fitzgerald was the Φ of the *New Monthly Magazine* at this date

* See vol. ii., p. 550 ; vol. iv., p. 26 and vol. x., p. 48.

cannot be positively asserted; but I believe he was an early contributor to its pages.*

In subsequent volumes of the magazine a more puzzling problem presents itself. Its editor from 1820 to 1829 was Thomas Campbell; and in 1825 his attention was drawn to the Φ poems in the *Morning Chronicle*, and especially to that on the London University (No. XIV. of Part I.), of which, as is well known, he was the most active promoter. In November of that year Praed mentions in a private letter that he had been asked to contribute to "Colburn's Magazine;" and accordingly within twelve months of that date there appeared four of his poems in its pages, the last of which, "Time's Song" (see vol. i. of the Collected Poems, p. 296), he signed with his old *Morning Chronicle* signature Φ. What follows is matter of conjecture. It is believed that this unintentional trespass, on his part, upon the sign-manual of another contributor, may have led to an introduction, to an acquaintance between the two, and to a merry agreement to dispute the possession of it, by *writing* for it in competition, under Thomas Campbell's banner. Certain it is, that about this time a friendship began between Praed and Fitzgerald, and that during the years 1827-9 no less than seventeen poems appear in the *New Monthly* which are signed with a "Phi," but with significant differences in the type. The first seven have a very small uncial Φ, from a different fount to that previously employed. Of these the first, "A Song of Impossibilities" (Part I., No. VI.) is obviously Praed's. The second, "Lines to the Fourteenth of February" (Collected Poems, vol. ii., p. 176) is, no doubt, by Praed also, possibly with

* See "Stanzas to Lord Edward Fitzgerald," signed F., vol. v., p. 351.

Fitzgerald's collaboration. The third I have no hesitation in ascribing to Fitzgerald alone. It contains all the distinguishing notes of his style.* Then follow three poems which are known to be Praed's: "Utopia" (see Part. I., No. XIX.) "Good-night to the Season" (Collected Poems, vol. ii., p. 183), the original MSS. of which, in Praed's handwriting, is in the possession of Sir Theodore Martin; and "My Partner" (Collected Poems, vol. ii., p. 150. The last of the seven signed with the small uncial Φ is "A Chapter of Ifs;" this is, in my opinion, by Fitzgerald, but possibly with Praed's collaboration. By this time Praed's right, by conquest, to the disputed initial may be considered to have become established; and in June 1828 an amicable partition appears to have been effected, Praed retaining the uncial Φ, which assumed its original goodly proportions, while Fitzgerald contented himself with the cursive φ. This arrangement held good till May 1829, when Bulwer Lytton became editor of the magazine, and the two friends simultaneously discontinued their contributions. In 1832, after Thomas Hood had succeeded to the editorship, Praed sent him one piece without a signature; he was now writing regularly in the Conservative press, and naturally had no wish to identify himself with his earlier *ego* of *Morning Chronicle* celebrity. Fitzgerald meanwhile used (or abused) the signature on many occasions. I have tracked him in

* The following is the best verse : the imitation of Praed is very close, but the grammar is weak, in two places :—

"I think of youth—its walks and rides
  O'er hills and trackless plains *together*,
 The charming disregard of guides,
  The sweet forgetfulness of weather;
 And that bright day, and that dark wood,
  Where love's long silence first was broken,
 In words not clearly understood,
  Because not very clearly spoken."

the *Literary Souvenir* for 1830 and 1831, in the *Gem* for 1831, in the *Morning Post* of January and February 1832, and in the *Court Journal* of the same period, sometimes signing Φ, sometimes φ, sometimes E, or F; and finally, in the *New Monthly* of 1837, during Theodore Hook's short editorship, he began a series over the initial Φ which continued with unabated vigour till some years after Praed's death. It is safe to say of these, as of all the "Phi" pieces which may be unearthed hereafter of later date than 1830, that Praed wrote no line of any of them. He may, however, have assisted Fitzgerald in some of his political pieces, written, as stated in my Notes on Part II., Nos. XXXVI., LII., for the *Morning Post* in 1833-5.

This theory of the distribution of the "Phi" poems, I had long ago worked out independently, chiefly from internal evidence. But I have since, by Sir Theodore Martin's kindness, been enabled to verify it, in a remarkable manner, by means of the autographs in his possession.

With the above-mentioned autograph poem of Praed's Sir Theodore Martin purchased another in a different handwriting, said to be that of Fitzgerald, "Praed's friend." It is called "Chivalry at a Discount," and was printed in the *New Monthly* for January 1829; and also in Mr. Locker Lampson's *Lyra Elegantiarum*. This poem, although signed with the cursive φ, has been attributed to Praed, erroneously indeed, but more plausibly than the rest of Fitzgerald's imitations, for, as Sir T. Martin's MS. shows, it was throughout corrected by Praed himself! The motto from Barry Cornwall is of his supplying; and an emendation in the last stanza presents so droll an example of the relations between the two friends, that it is worth while to quote it. Fitzgerald had written :—

"Oh had I lived in those bright times,
Fair Cousin, for thy glances—
Instead of many senseless rhymes—
I had been breaking lances!"

The grammar of which is not more faulty than the sentiment is trite. Praed corrects—and the little round text characters seem to laugh in our faces as they run :—

"Oh, had I in those times been bred,
Fair Cousin, for thy glances—
Instead of *breaking Priscian's head*,
I had been breaking lances!"

With which may be compared, from the "Eve of Battle" (Collected Poems, vol. ii., p. 11),

"On, on! take forts and storm positions!
Break Frenchmen's heads, *instead of Priscian's*."

The composition is signed with an erased initial, apparently a cursive Greek ξ, but imperfectly formed; and also by a badly formed φ. There are appended two inscriptions, by way of direction to the printer; the first is in Praed's handwriting: "Signature same as Mr. Praed's, but *small letter* instead of *capital;*" the second is in Charles Knight's, and runs thus: "φ 🖉 This CK. Keep out for next month the last of Mr. Praed's sent by me with the proof of sheet 3rd. CK." This requires a short explanation; Knight was at the time editing the *London Magazine* (see his *Passages of a Working Life*, vol. ii., pp. 67, 109); and to the third volume of the third series of it, the last that ever appeared, both Praed and Fitzgerald largely contributed. In this periodical, as

Knight himself informed me, they used for signatures to their poetry the Greek letters Ξ and ξ. Knight marked the pieces for me, from memory, in an American copy, and, as I have found by comparison, gave Praed those only which were signed with the uncial Ξ. Now in July 1829 the *London* was merged in the *New Monthly*; and while this transaction was in contemplation it seems that Knight must have been exercising a power to transfer contributions from the one to the other, and was probably engaged on the editing of both. A prose paper in the *New Monthly* for January 1829, " First Friendships," is easily to be identified as of Knight's own writing.

I subjoin a list of the pieces which have been, by Mr. Whitmore and others, attributed to Praed, and are, in all probability, by Fitzgerald.* Mr Whit-

* From the *New Monthly Magazine.*—" A Chapter of Ifs "; " The Light o' Love "; " Chivalry at a Discount "; " Song to a Serenader in February "; " Sybil's Letter "; " Cousins "; " A Classical Walk "; " Stanzas " (The songs she sung); " Because "; " The Conjuror "; " Stanzas " (Look down, etc.); " The Forsaken "; " Bagatelles," and eight charades. Praed wrote no charades in this magazine.

From the *London Magazine.*—" The Separation "; " Stanzas to ——"; " Hobbledehoys "; " Stanzas to——"; " Dreams "; " Good-night."

From the *Literary Souvenir.*—" An Invitation "; " Chivalry at a Discount " (another poem with this title).

Source Undetected.—" Confessions from the MS. of a Sexagenarian "; " An Old-fashioned Recipe." Mr. Whitmore also prints a mass of " Doubtful Pieces," by himself and others, in an Appendix, which he cannot seriously wish any one to suppose are Praed's. " A Letter from Miss A. Mortimer to Sir H. Clifton " (*N. M. M.*, vol. xxviii., p. 214), is obviously Irish in origin; but not, I think, good enough for Fitzgerald. It is probably to be attributed to a perpetrator of other execranda in the same pages, who signed himself O'C. The " Sonnet to Ada," by mistake assigned to Praed in the third edition of *The Etonian*, was by Chauncey Hare Townshend.

more has further called attention to the publication of two of Praed's songs, "with music by Mrs. E. M. Fitzgerald." She was an amateur singer of some considerable attraction; and the songs mentioned, with some others, were written for her piano.

I trust I have succeeded in leaving no excuse for ascribing Fitzgerald's imitations to Praed. Internal evidence might have been relied on, even without the external, to establish the same conclusions. But internal evidence will never prevent hasty critics from reviving a fallacy. As a proof that Praed's fame has suffered from the ascription to him of a mass of verse which is unworthy of him, I may adduce some smart lines, written by the late Mr. Mortimer Collins, and circulated by him as Praed's, by way of a joke. There was no great harm in this, if the verses had been a good imitation of Praed; but, as a fact, they are only an imitation of the imitation; very fair "Fitzgerald," but very unfair "Praed."

There are indications in his writings that Praed was not under any delusions as to the limitations of his own genius. He is not, and never supposed himself to be, among the greater singers. He wrote to please, and pleased by simple means. His limitations are, however, partly self-imposed. He might easily have raised a coarser laugh, or have inflicted an empoisoned wound. He turned away from such triumphs, and refused such praise. It is only his due that his muse should be cleared from the discredit of inferior work, in which there is much that his taste would have rejected, and much more that his judgment would have condemned. Only after such a process of sifting can his readers be in a position fairly to estimate his merits.

Of those merits it is no part of my intention to write

at length. They are of a character not easy to be missed. Since Ovid, with the exception of Pope, there has been no such fluency of versification, no such ingenuity of poetical rhetoric. As a writer of political satire Praed does not enter the lists with Swift and Marvel; still less does he cope with Juvenal; he is among the light horsemen, of whom Horace is unapproachably the first. Here, however, he is first among English writers; before Prior, before Canning, before the authors of the Rolliad, and far before Moore or any of the still anonymous contributors to the later London Press. Satire of this kind is out of fashion now. Our present minor poets have one great fault, that they want too often to be major poets. The themes they choose, the styles they affect, require fuller inspiration. The lower walks of poetry, abandoned by the cleverest, are invaded in turn by scribblers and rhymesters, who have neither the industry to learn how to make verses, nor the ear to recognize a verse when it is made. Our politics suffer from this cause. Party spirit becomes more sombre, when its humorous side is not brought into prominence. Hypocrisy and Puffery might be not so immodest, if occasionally scarified by the lash of Thalia. In the absence of humour we become abusive. More satire would sweeten the air of controversy. It is a mistake to suppose that satire is necessarily unamiable; a satirist is not the same as a cynic. These are some of the reflections suggested by a perusal of such pages as follow. Those who do not agree with them will at least agree in this—that the book is, emphatically, an amusing book.

POLITICAL AND OCCASIONAL POEMS.

PART I.

1823—1830.

I.

A FREE TRANSLATION OF A LETTER FROM PRINCE HILT TO A FRIEND AT PARIS.

[This earliest that I have found of Praed's Political Poems appeared in the *Morning Chronicle* of 7th Aug., 1823, signed ⴲ. It occurs fairly transcribed in an original MSS. book of the poet's, containing, among other things, the earliest copy of "Lillian." There are some slight variations from the published copy, which appear to be corrections.

" Prince Hilt " is the Duc d' Angoulême, elder son of Charles X., and nephew of Louis XVIII. On the 7th April this prince passed the Bidassoa at the head of a French army of 100,000 men, and invaded Spain, in collusion with its monarch, Ferdinand VII., for the purpose of suppressing the Spanish " Constitution of 1812," which had been re-established in 1820, as the result of the insurrection of Riego, and of the treachery of O'Donnel. The Holy Alliance, instituted by the Czar Alexander after the fall of Napoleon, and joined by Ferdinand in 1817, was at the bottom of this aggression, which had been resolved upon at the Congress of Verona. The Spanish Ministry, taking the king along with them, retired to Seville. On May 23rd the French main body entered Madrid; but the left wing, under Marshal Moncey, experienced much resistance in Catalonia from the Guerrilla forces under Mina, and was effectually prevented from taking part in the advance. Soon, however, O'Donnel, at the head of the national forces, again betrayed his employers, and declared for submission to the French demands; but being met with some indignation from his own officers, he fled privately from his head quarters,

POLITICAL AND OCCASIONAL POEMS.

and joined the invaders. The king was thereupon carried off to Cadiz, which was soon afterwards besieged. O'Donnel's example of treason was on June 26 followed by General Morillo, to whom the chief command had been entrusted in the north of Spain; and although he was abandoned by all but a very small force, his defection took away all heart for further resistance from the Constitutional Army. Riego became a fugitive, was captured, and ultimately hanged. On the 31st August, the Trocadero, an outwork of Cadiz, was surprised; and the war ended, Oct. 1, with the surrender of Cadiz. The attitude of England, in the later days of Lord Liverpool's administration, with Canning for foreign minister, was one of disgusted neutrality.]

FROM climate hot and hot campaign
   I write, *ma chère amie*,
To let you know how nobly Spain
   Agrees with France and me;
All folks misled by false pretences
Recover now their chains, and senses,
   And all the crowds I see
Adore, without the slightest shyness,
The Inquisition, and my Highness.

Whene'er we meet a whiskered foe
   He's sure to be defeated,
(My bulletins have told you so)
   Yet corpses have retreated;
And every day the battle-slain,
Substantial ghosts, start up again,
   And Hell and I are cheated,
And blade and ball begin to soften,
We kill the brutes so very often!

A FREE TRANSLATION OF A LETTER.

We pass our time delightfully;
   I like, as I'm a sinner,
My laurels after victory,
   My claret after dinner;
Yet mirth and meat are very dear,
And pursuivant and pioneer
   Are looking rather thinner;
And though I love the Spanish ladies,
I wish they'd let us into Cadiz.

I also like Madrid nobility
   Where Dons and Dames abound,
And patronize Madrid civility
   Where drums and Vivas sound;
I also like the Friars and Nuns,
The cowls, the Canons—not the guns—
   And look in rapture round
When all the Counts and all their wives
Damn the Guerrillas and their knives.

The peasantry seem quite content;
   The King has got the gout;
The Cortez seem securely pent—
   The devil may drive them out!
Old Moncey has been often bit;
But he has length of beard and wit,
   And knows what he's about;
While Mina swears in every weather,
And cuts his jokes and throats together.

You know O'Donnel's plot was blown;
　　And General Morillo
Might just as well have left alone
　　His little peccadillo.
They did not, sweetest love, amuse,
And were not of the smallest use;
　　And I must wear the willow,
And mourn that two such glorious traitors
Could only bring their grins and gaiters.

Adieu! you'll understand my story
　　From this right royal rhyme;
I've gained a deal of ground and glory,
　　And lost a deal of time.
My uniform is much admired:
(I'm getting wonderfully tired)
　　My boots are quite sublime;
And I remember in my prayer
Paris—kid gloves—*et vous ma chère!*

II.
CHANCERY MORALS.

[Side by side with the last poem there appeared, in the next column of the *Morning Chronicle*, notices of an article in the current number of the *Edinburgh Review*, criticising some recent equity decisions by Lord Eldon in matters of copyright. By these decisions it had been established that no protection would be given to copyright by way of injunction, where the contents of the work were calculated to do injury to the public, or to contradict the doctrines of the Scriptures. Under the second head was decided, in 1822, the case of Murray *v.* Benbow, where the work pirated was Byron's "Cain." Under the first an injunction was dissolved, during this year, which had been granted by Vice-Chancellor Gifford, to restrain a pirated edition of "Don Juan." Other works to which protection was on similar grounds refused, were Wolcot's "Peter Pindar," Southey's " Wat Tyler," and the Physiological Lectures of Sir W. Lawrence, delivered at the College of Surgeons; these last on the ground that the Chancellor "entertained a doubt, he thought a rational doubt," whether they were not inconsistent with the doctrine of the immortality of the soul. See Jacob's *Chancery Reports*, p. 474.

This poem appeared in the same paper, with the same signature as the last, on August 12, 1823; and is also transcribed, with a few emendations, in the MSS. book above noticed.—Of the booksellers mentioned, Carlile was the subject of several prosecutions for blasphemous and indecent publications, and was at the time undergoing a sentence of fine and imprisonment, for reprinting Paine's "Age of Reason," and Elihu Palmer's "Principles of

Nature."—The " fence " is, of course, the receiver of stolen goods. It used to cause some laughter in court, when Lord Eldon solemnly announced that "he had read" the objectionable volume.]

> "Round, around, about, about, about :
> All ill come running in, all good keep out."—*Macbeth*.

BOLD Benbow rubs his jovial eyes,
    And lauds the Law's refinement ;
Dense Dugdale is in ecstasies,
    Though Carlile's in confinement ;
And guilt hath wed legality ;
    And useful through the nation
Is prurience to publicity
    And sin to circulation.
" Don Juan was a horrid beast,
    And that was why we selled 'un : "
So say the Statutes ; or at least
    So says the Earl of Eldon.

Pert Poll has come from Kentish Town
    With sixpence in her pocket,
Red Rose has sold her yellow gown,
    Meek Meg her little locket,
And Molly, who with Mrs. Fry
    Has crammed a deal of cant, goes
To pawn her prayers for poetry,
    Her canticles for Cantos.
" ' Don Juan ' is a very feast,
    So wicked 'tis and well done,

We thank Heav'n for it—or at least
  We thank the Earl of Eldon!"

The City hath its myriads sent
  To learn what Byron's pen does,
And bakers study sentiment,
  And butchers innuendoes;
And big Bow bells unheeded chime,
  And Beaux and Belles grow tender;
And Taste admires a double rhyme
  And *Ton* a *double entendre;*
And frail ones, whose illicit trade
  Could never else have held on,
Cry "Bless my soul! our fortune's made!
  Long live the Earl of Eldon!"

The girls of the Academy,
  With empty heads and purses,
Bless Charity and Chancery
  For cheapening naughty verses;
And Mauds and Marys peep and pay
  With sigh and shilling ready,
And Anna envies " Julia,"
  And Araminta " Haidee";
And *Gouvernantes* are furious quite—
  "Lord! what have Bet and Bell done?
They've read 'Don Juan' through to-night,
  And blest the Earl of Eldon!"

Bad Byron loathes the legal Fence,
 The guardian of good order,
The conqueror of common sense
 From Cornwall to the Border;
And damns his doubts and his delays,
 His quibbles and quotations,
His knowing nods and solemn says,
 His robes and revelations.
" This piracy will never do !
 I'll send you down to Hell, Don;
The *devils* have a right to you—
 So says the Earl of Eldon."

III.
LETTERS TO ILLUSTRIOUS CHARACTERS.

I.—A COMPLIMENTARY EPISTLE TO THE EMPEROR OF RUSSIA.

[From the *Morning Chronicle* of 1st Sept., 1823, signed Φ. Whatever respect for the Czar Alexander the events of 1814 might have left in the minds of Englishmen was entirely obliterated by the Franco-Spanish War. The first and last stanzas of this epistle have, however, a satiric intention reflecting upon some one nearer home than Russia; some one to whom Tierney's speeches and Canning's frets were of more moment than they could possibly be to a Romanoff, without any Parliamentary Opposition to bother him.—Pozzo di Borgo, the Corsican employed by Russia as Ambassador at Paris, and Tierney, the not very brilliant leader of the Whig Opposition, are already almost forgotten; and the circumstances that Alexander was at one time suspected of complicity in his father's murder, and that he had recently issued a ukase to prevent any report being published in Russia of the trial of Carlile, may be noticed, in explanation of the elaborate sneers that are bestowed upon him.]

GREAT Sire, since Princes sometimes ask—
For Princes are but men—
Respite from table and from task,
From Petersburg's enlivening flask
And Pozzo's patent pen,

Don't give your Royal brain the vapours
By opening Opposition papers ;
Leave Prince and Parliament alone,
To squabble for their barren bone ;
While Pittites pout and Foxites fume,
And Mr. Peel drubs Mr. Hume,
Mind only how your Guards are laced,
And pinch your subjects, and your waist,
And put embroidery on your breeches,
And read no more of Tierney's speeches.

For me, I am a loyal wight,
   And love to flatter Princes ;
The Treasury triumphs when I write,
   And all the faction winces ;
And I am going to compare
Your father's honourable heir
With Philip's less resplendent son,
The glory of old Macedon.
Look very grand and very gracious,
And smooth your brow and your mustachios,
And let a would-be Laureate tell a
Few stories of the Prince of Pella.

Philip and Paul, your sire and his,
   Both found a gory bier ;
He shed the murderers' blood for this,
   And you—the mourner's tear ;

He rooted up, you down—the weed;
    And sage was your adviser,
For his might be the holier deed,
    But yours was far the wiser;
Your boasting, like his bowl, mounts high;
    He poured his long libations
As quickly as your Majesty
    Can pour your protestations;
And Greece was ever fond of whim,
    And fond of falsehood too,
And, as she swallowed wine for him,
    She swallows lies for you.
Both made a bonfire in the land,
    For love's—or glory's lures;
Sweet Thais lit the Grecian brand,
    And sour Rostopchin yours.
Your torch was dipped in grief and gore,
    And his in mirth and laughter;
He drank a drop or two before,
    You wept as many after.
You both were swift in letting blood,
    And both were swift in swearing,
And, if he passed Granicus' flood,
    Why, you have passed all bearing;
So both have made a monstrous fuss,
    And made the barbers prate,
And you are dubbed Magnanimous,
    And he was voted Great.

And lauded and bespattered thus
   By gazers and by gapers,
He lies in his sarcophagus,
   And you—in your state-papers.

And so farewell! Live on, in all
   That decks a crown with gladness,
In tented field and tapestried hall,
   In majesty and madness;
Enjoy the tailor's cunning toil,
And patronize Macassar Oil,
And never heed how Canning frets,
And plan your soldiers' epaulettes;
And sleep, begirt by vows and verses,
And bowing Counts, and bitter curses.

IV.
LETTERS TO ILLUSTRIOUS CHARACTERS.

II.—TO LA DESIRÉE OF LE DESIRÉ.

[*Morning Chronicle*, 23rd Sept., 1823, signed Φ. The particular fair one who was the much admired, at this juncture, of the elderly Monarch, Louis XVIII. of France, was apparently Madame Du Cayla.—The town of Cadiz was still invested, though the chance of its holding out long was infinitesimal.—Talleyrand, created Prince of Benevento by Napoleon, had been Bishop of Autun before the Revolution; and was considered likely, old as he was, to survive the restored monarchy—as indeed he actually did.—Lafayette, after being the hero of one stage of the Revolution, and very nearly the victim of another, had been kept for some time very safely in an Austrian prison, and had lived quietly while Napoleon was in power; but he was now figuring away at a great rate as an Opposition leader, and shortly afterwards found it prudent to make a starring tour in the United States.]

Fair Lady, from whose lips and eyes
The Royal Bourbon snatches
Oblivion of rebellious cries,
Thick legs and thicker Deputies,
Short wit and long despatches,
Sweet Sorceress, at whose smile or frown,
The Father of all France

Sinks all the sorrows of the Crown,
And leaves the Duke to take the town,
  Or else—to take his chance;
Forgive me if I dare intrude
  On your exalted station,
And venture—I was always rude—
To greet you in your solitude
  With song and salutation.

Queen of the play-house and the Press,
  Of operas and of odes,
Supreme o'er dances and o'er dress,
All-influencing patroness
  Of ministers and modes,
'Tis yours—'tis yours to bring again
Legitimacy's glorious reign,
And fill again the arms of kings
With *liaisons* and twenty things
Which fled in horror from the scene
Of *Sansculotte* and *Guillotine*.

Yours is the great and varied sway
Which politics and pins obey;
Yours is the empire, as is fit,
O'er Church and Senate, war and wit,
Curés and canons, marshals, misses,
Cards, compliments, charades, and kisses,
The soldier's sash, the poet's dream,
New bonnets, and the old *régime*.

The fair and faded Marquis flies
   To tell his griefs to you,
With dingy coat and twitching eyes,
Cold sentiments and burning sighs,
   Long stories and long *queue*.
To you the happy author brings
   His dry though dripping sheet,
And reads, and raves, and swears, and sings,
And eulogizes limping kings
   In very limping feet;
And advocates fill up the crowd
Immensely ignorant and loud,
And officers with bloodless blades,
Who practise grins and gasconnades,
And doat on laces and liqueur,
Love, glory, and the *Moniteur;*
And the Prince-Prelate—for he knows
How all the pageant comes and goes,
Looks on in silence all the while
With shaking head and quiet smile,
And smothers, till a proper season,
His studied jest and plotted treason.

Thrice blest is he for whom you deck
   Your boudoir and your curls,
For whom you clothe your snowy neck
   In perfumes and in pearls;

Thrice blest, for he remembers not
   That horrible Convention,
The perils of his exiled lot,
   His patrons, and his pension;
And Spain is low, and *Rentes* are high,
   In spite of Lafayette;
And Paris is in ecstasy,
   And England is in debt;
And Soult and Suchet fret and grieve,
And pretty *Poissardes* bellow " *Vive!* "
And Murder sleeps in St. Helena,
And Moncey is besieging Mina;
And that dark day can ne'er come back,
When stars and ribbands went to wrack,
When Gallia lost her lord and master,
And Peace fled fast, and he fled faster;
And all the fops who drank and dressed,
And wore a trinket at the breast,
In peril of their life and limb,
Packed up their trunks, and followed him.

V.

LOVE'S ETERNITY.

[This is the earliest poem of a type often afterwards repeated by Praed, in which a strain of social compliment, or a mere verbal tune, is made the setting for as many allusions to personages or topics of the day as it seemed good to the versifier to introduce. " Patter-songs " they may be called ; but they are, at all events, very good patter. It appeared in the *Morning Chronicle* of 6th May, 1824, and was quoted to me by Charles Knight as " by your uncle." It has the same signature, Φ, as the preceding series.—For Carlile, see No. II. above.—The *John Bull*, edited by Theodore Hook, is repeatedly attacked in these pieces for its indecency and scurrility.—The Tenth Hussars, afterwards Lord Cardigan's regiment, were notable for their cherry-coloured breeches, George IV.'s army-tailoring masterpiece.—Hoops had to wait thirty years, before the Empress Eugénie brought them "in" again.—Bankes, though a dull writer, and a strong partisan of the No-popery school, was not more dishonest than other Tories—or Whigs ; but he was Tory member for Cambridge University, and therefore more obnoxious than others to an undergraduate Liberal.—Alexander Baring, afterwards Lord Ashburton, was one of those eminent authorities on finance, who are eminently uncongenial to light-hearted rhymesters.—Mr. Martin, the member for Galway, was a standing joke in the House, but did good service to humanity with some of his numerous Bills to prevent Cruelty to Animals.—Mr. Cobbett, editor of the ultra-Radical *Weekly Register*, got in, like other Radicals, in 1832.—The ladies mentioned in the last couplet were famous—or otherwise—in their day.]

"Cum Paris Enone potuit sperare relicta
Ad fontem Xanthi versa recurrit aqua."—OVID.

What need of wit ? What need of wile ?
    I know your eyes are killing ;
But oh ! he isn't worth a smile,
    Who isn't worth a shilling !
And yet, by all the gods of rhyme,
    And by your lips I swear,
Though all my love is loss of time
    And all my hope despair,
The glittering stream shall cease to stray,
    The wind refuse to rove,
All solid things shall melt away,
    Before I cease to love !

Fair Freedom shall be found in Quod,
    Stern Justice in the Quorum,
Carlile shall praise the grace of God,
    John Bull shall learn decorum,
Loyal addresses shall omit
    " Our fortunes and our lives,"
The Commons shall be famed for wit,
    The Lords for virtuous wives,
The Tenth shall dress without a glass
    Or dine with one remove,
All monstrous things shall come to pass
    Before I cease to love.

Young widowhood shall lose its weeds,
    Old kings shall loathe the Tories,
And monks be tired of telling beads,
    And blues of telling stories ;
And titled suitors shall be crossed,
    And famished poets married,
And Canning's motion shall be lost
    And Hume's amendment carried,
And Chancery shall cease to doubt,
    And Algebra to prove,
And hoops come in, and gas go out,
    Before I cease to love.

And Peel shall sink his Popery-cry,
    And Buxton lay his plans down,
And Bankes shall vote with honesty,
    And Liverpool with Lansdowne ;
And hungry knights shall lose their steak
    And never talk of pairing,
And county members keep awake
    Through half an hour of Baring :
And not a soul shall go to grin
    When Martin goes to move,
And Mr. Cobbett shall get in,
    Before I cease to love !

Good sense shall go to Parliament,
    The tithe shall be abated,

A Papist shall be innocent,
    A slave emancipated,
A French gallant shall break his heart,
    A Spanish Count his fetters,
A fortune-teller trust her art,
    A Radical his betters;
A pretty face shall like a veil,
    A pretty hand a glove,
And Reason win, and bribery fail,
    Before I cease to love.

In short, the world shall all go mad,
    And saints shall take to masquing,
And kisses and estates be had
    For nothing but the asking;
And beauty shall be ugliness,
    And ocean shall be dry,
And passion shall be passionless
    And truth itself a lie,
And "Stars" shall cease to shine below,
    And stars to shine above,
And Cunningham be left for Lowe,
    Before I cease to love.

VI.

A SONG OF IMPOSSIBILITIES.

[Appeared in the January number for 1827 of the *New Monthly Magazine*, and has been preferred to this place, in order that it may follow directly on the last. The signature again is Φ, which was being used by Praed, when he wrote this, in common with E. M. Fitzgerald.—The lime-tree avenue of Trinity College, planted 1717, is still famous.—Sir Thomas Buckler Lethbridge of Sandhill Park, a typical squire from Somerset, represented his county for more than twenty years. The stiffer Tories were deaf to the anti-protectionist ideas, of which Mr. Huskisson was the representative in the Ministry.—Mr. Sumner stood for Surrey unsuccessfully at the General Election of May 1826.—Mr. Bankes (see No. V.) had written a book of his travels in the East, for which James Silk Buckingham did the plates, and afterwards republished them, in " Travels " of his own.—Mr. Henry Bishop, afterwards knighted, the representative of the English School in music, produced in 1826 his grand opera of *Aladdin*, by way of rivalry with Weber's *Oberon*. Its failure may be said to have definitely established his position as a second-rate composer.—Theatrical performances being prohibited within the limits of the Vice-Chancellor's authority, the study of *Tom Thumb*, Fielding's burlesque tragedy, was of less frequency among gentlemen at college in those days, than it has been since Mr. Burnand founded the A.D.C.—Dr. Geldart was Professor of Civil Law at Cambridge; what slip in scholarship had thrown doubt upon his knowledge of Greek, I have not been able to ascertain.—In the great commercial crisis of December 1825, the first bank to break was that of Sir W.

Pole and Co., December 5. The next day that of Messrs. Williams followed the example, but this firm eventually resumed payment, mainly in consequence of Mr. Henry Thornton's support, who was connected with the firm.—Mr. Const had been for many years Chairman of the Middlesex Magistrates, and might be supposed to have outlived all illusions on the subject of "highly honourable" rogues.—The Right Hon. Charles Watkin Wynn, second son of Sir Watkin, and grandson of George Grenville, was at this time President of the Board of Control. Praed writes under date 22nd Feb., 1830, "The great Duke complains bitterly of the inefficiency of the Treasury Corps; and says, with oaths that I will not shock you by repeating, 'Privy Councillors ought to speak,—'Privy Councillors OUGHT to speak!'"—Grecian scrip was not very likely to rise, after the treatment which the Greeks received from their friends; for which see Moore's "Ghost of Miltiades," directed against Joseph Hume:—

> He runs to tell how hard his lot is
> To Messrs. Orlando and Luriotti's,
> And says, "O Greece, for Liberty's sake
> Do buy my scrip, and I vow to break
> Those dark unholy bonds of thine—
> If you'll only consent to buy up mine!"]

"Ici finit le roman; où l'on remarquera que je ne suis pas heureux dans la conclusion de mes amours."—ROUSSEAU.

LADY, I loved you all last year,
   How honestly and well—
Alas! would weary you to hear,
   And torture me to tell;
I raved beneath the midnight sky,
   I sang beneath the limes—
Orlando in my lunacy,
   And Petrarch in my rhymes.
But all is over! When the sun
   Dries up the boundless main,

When black is white, false-hearted one,
  I may be yours again!

When passion's early hopes and fears
  Are not derided things;
When truth is found in falling tears,
  Or faith in golden rings;
When the dark Fates that rule our way
  Instruct me where they hide
One woman that would ne'er betray,
  One friend that never lied;
When summer shines without a cloud,
  And bliss without a pain;
When worth is noticed in a crowd,
  I may be yours again!

When science pours the light of day
  Upon the lords of lands;
When Huskisson is heard to say
  That Lethbridge understands;
When wrinkles work their way in youth,
  Or Eldon's in a hurry;
When lawyers represent the truth,
  Or Mr. Sumner Surrey;
When aldermen taste eloquence
  Or bricklayers champagne;
When common law is common sense,
  I may be yours again

When learned judges play the beau,
    Or learned pigs the tabor;
When traveller Bankes beats Cicero,
    Or Mr. Bishop Weber;
When Sinking Funds discharge a debt,
    Or female hands a bomb;
When bankrupts study the *Gazette*,
    Or colleges *Tom Thumb;*
When little fishes learn to speak,
    Or poets not to feign;
When Dr. Geldart construes Greek,
    I may be yours again!

When Pole and Thornton honour cheques,
    Or Mr. Const a rogue;
When Jericho's in Middlesex,
    Or minuets in vogue;
When Highgate goes to Devonport,
    Or fashion to Guildhall;
When argument is heard at Court,
    Or Mr. Wynn at all;
When Sidney Smith forgets to jest,
    Or farmers to complain;
When kings that are are not the best,
    I may be yours again!

When peers from telling money shrink,
    Or monks from telling lies;

A SONG OF IMPOSSIBILITIES.

When hydrogen begins to sink,
   Or Grecian scrip to rise;
When German poets cease to dream,
   Americans to guess;
When Freedom sheds her holy beam
   On Negroes, and the Press;
When there is any fear of Rome,
   Or any hope of Spain;
When Ireland is a happy home,
   I may be yours again!

When you can cancel what has been,
   Or alter what must be,
Or bring once more that vanished scene,
   Those withered joys, to me;
When you can tune the broken lute,
   Or deck the blighted wreath,
Or rear the garden's richest fruit,
   Upon a blasted heath;
When you can lure the wolf at bay
   Back to his shattered chain,
To-day may then be yesterday—
   I may be yours again!

VII.
ODE TO THE CHANCELLOR.

IMITATED FROM HORACE, III., XV.

[From the *Morning Chronicle* of 14th Feb., 1825, signed Φ. Praed took his degree about this time, and was already beginning to "eat dinners" at the Middle Temple. This Ode appears to have been the fruit of a first visit to the precincts of the Law, where the extravagant delays of Lord Eldon, now not more than 74 years of age, but occupied chiefly in nursing his reputation as a judge, and in political intrigue, would be the common topic at the students' table; and the singular aptitude of legal "shop" for punning purposes could not fail to strike a punster.—Robinson, afterwards Lord Goderich, was now Chancellor of the Exchequer.— Lord Eldon's grudging distribution of the coveted "silk gown," the emblem of the dignity of a King's Counsel, was especially noticeable in the case of Whig aspirants. His long tenure of the Woolsack had effectually blocked the highest step in the ladder of legal promotion; but some amends had been made to the Bar by the institution in 1813 of the office of Vice-Chancellor, and in 1823 Lord Gifford was appointed Deputy-Speaker in the Lords, for the sake of improving the Appeal Tribunal. There is a formidable indictment of Lord Eldon, on the ground of his procrastinations, in the *Edinburgh Review* for October 1823; the topic was from this time forward never long without mention in the press; in 1824 the conduct of the attacks passed from Mr. Michael Angelo Taylor, who was hardly *un homme sérieux*, to Mr. John Williams; and in 1827 a hostile vote in the Commons, followed by the substitution of Canning for Liverpool as Prime Minister, forced the unwilling Chancellor to resign.]

ODE TO THE CHANCELLOR.

[1] OLD Lady of Chancery, why do you tarry
   So long on the throne of your vanishing reign?
The neighbourhood titters whene'er you miscarry,
   And hints that your labours are labours in vain.

There is one thing at least, which your closest endeavour
   Will hardly discover a reason to doubt,
That be candles and statesmen how wicked soever,
   All candles and statesmen at last must go out.

When girls in their summer begin to grow willing,
   Their grandmothers think about making their wills;
And oh, you had better be done with your billing,
   Before your old lovers say "no" to your bills!

'Tis all very pretty, when love or defiance
   Is breathed from the lips of a younger coquette;
When Peel is seduced by the Holy Alliance,
   Or Robinson flirts with the National Debt.

[2] But it is not for you, when the grave gapes before you,
   To be scaring gilt stars with those wrinkles of awe;

   [1] Uxor pauperis Ibyci,
      Tandem nequitiæ fige modum tuæ,
   Famosisque laboribus.

   Maturo propior desine funeri
     . . . . .
   —— stellis nebulam spargere candidis.

Giving garters and ribbands to fools who adore you,
    And stealing silk gowns from your daughters-in-law.

[1] Sweet Gifford, I grant, as your tenderness taught her,
    May flaunt in rich suits, and be kind to appeals;
And dabble her scull in the dirtiest water,
    Like a Greenlander, all for the love of the seals;

[2] But you—put your salary up in your full sack,
    And go to your grave with a gentle decline;
Take a nightcap of woollens instead of a wool-sack,
    And leave to George Canning his roses and wine.

---

[1]   ——filia rectius
  Expugnat juvenum domos;
  .   .   .   .   .
  Illam cogit amor Nothi
    Lascivæ similem ludere capreæ.

  Te lanæ prope nobilem
    Tonsæ Luceriam, non citharæ, decent.

VIII.
WISDOM OF THE GREAT COUNCIL. I.

[*Morning Chronicle*, 17 February, 1825, signed Φ. On the 10th February Mr. Goulburn, as Secretary to the Lord Lieutenant, moved to bring in a "Bill to suppress unlawful Associations in Ireland," directed against the Catholic Association. The speech is a tedious one, and this parody of it is helped out with lights from other speakers. Thus the second stanza is from Canning; "Self-elected, self-constituted, self-assembled, self-adjourned, acknowledging no superior, tolerating no equal, interfering in all stages with the administration of justice," denouncing individuals, menacing the press, levying contributions—"the House was justified in saying it should exist no longer." It was an object with the Ministerial speakers to establish that the Association was virtually of a representative character, since this peculiarity would, if it had been accorded, have brought it within the ban of the existing law. At the same time, stress was laid upon its representing one opinion only; Mr. Goulburn enlarged upon this, and upon its imitation of the powers of Parliament; also upon the collection of the so-called "Rent," and upon outrages, abetted or only hypocritically discountenanced by the chiefs of the Association. Peel and Plunkett spoke on the same side. Among such colleagues, taking diametrically opposite views on the main question of Catholic Emancipation, there could not but be a good deal of firing into each other's ranks; and in the travesty of their arguments which follows full advantage has been taken of the circumstance. Thus Plunkett seemed to allow that "the intentions of the Association were *now* honest and peaceable;" and when to this was added the admission necessary in order to make out a case for legislation, that there was "nothing illegal" in the Association, so far as concerned its avowed proceedings, as the law then stood, it is easy to see that room was left for a telling rejoinder in debate. The operation of the Bill was limited to three years, a short-sighted provision; and in 1828 the Association was revived accordingly, and speedily brought matters to a crisis.—The Catholic Rent was a subscription of one penny per month, collected chiefly through the agency of the parish priests, and handed over to O'Connell, to be expended at his discretion. It was paid in this form by about half a million of Irishmen, and was largely supplemented by subscriptions of one guinea per annum from the wealthier Catholics.—Mr. Butterworth, the law publisher in Fleet Street, was Treasurer of the Wesleyan Methodist Connexion, one of the founders of the Bible Society, and M.P. for Dover. Among Nonconformists he took a leading part in opposition to the Catholic claims. He was the son of a Lancashire Baptist minister, and any connexion between him and Lutterworth must have been nominal merely.—The *gravamen* is the technical name given to a grievance, viewed as the subject for a resolution in the Lower House of Convocation.]

"ERE our measures we move, our facts we must
    prove,"
  Says the solemn official Goulburn;
And proceeds with grave face to establish his case,
  Like a meagre octavo from Colburn:
Undertaking to show that a vigorous blow,
  Struck home by the heads of the nation,
In the name of the Crown, ought at once to put
    down
    The Catholic Association.

"Sir, they never were sent to misrepresent
  Our counties, ports, boroughs and cities;

Yet they constantly ape our voice, manner and
    shape,
  Standing orders and standing committees;
Self-convoked, self-returned, self-controlled, self-
    adjourned,
  Without more than six weeks' vacation,
They make such a fuss, not a soul cares for *Us*:
  This impudent Association!

" How freely they sent their Catholic " Rent "
  (A Popish misnomer for taxing),
While Robinson burns at their easy returns
  Who pocket the money for *axing!*
Very true, they're not willing to part with a
    shilling;
  Their subscriptions are mere affectation,
By menaces made up—though readily paid up—
  Hypocritical Association!

" Our reliance how just, that the law we could trust
  For protecting our wives and our daughters—
Though we very well know, only three years ago
  Ireland lay like a log on the waters!
What monsters are those, who dare interpose
  In our criminal administration!
Though all the committed are tried—and acquitted;
  What a culpable Association!

"Sir, turning from Law, we must listen with awe
    To the sounds of confusion and riot;
But if all tamely sit, and in silence submit—
    They are still more alarming when quiet!
Of all evils accurst, civil war is the worst,
    And fiery insubordination!
Better bloodshed and rout, than a peace brought about
    By this damnable Association!

"Sir, I hold that the priests are no better than beasts—
    In spite of some trifling varieties;
And beg to disclaim all this fury and flame
    On the part of the Bible Societies.
The Ass in the Fable was quite as much able
    In Heaven to produce agitation,
As aught this side Hell—but the soul-shaking bell
    Of the Catholic Association!

"Without throwing dirt, I most fully assert—
    Contradict me who dare or who can, Sir—
That our foes are plunged in incompatible sin!
    Let the votes of this House give the answer
Most humble, yet proudest—most silent, yet loudest—
    The greatest—and least—in creation,

The strongest—the weakest, the fiercest—the meekest,
Is the Catholic Association.

"We must check by main force their dangerous course,
Put them down by the sword of the Law, Sir!
But if our Act fail, our mere wish will prevail,
And our enemies, bowing, withdraw—Sir!"
He ceased. Mr. Butterworth, a preacher from Lutterworth,
Stood as clerk to his clear predication;
Most pious of laymen, he groaned a *grave Amen!*
So good-night to the Association!

IX.

WISDOM OF THE GREAT COUNCIL. II.

[The famous speech of the Duke of York, 25th April 1825, on presenting a petition against Sir F. Burdett's Catholic Relief Bill, is not unfairly parodied in the following poem, which appeared in the *Morning Chronicle*, 9th June, 1825. It was so rash and ill-considered an effusion, that a revised edition had to be substituted; and even in this form it produced a great popular effect, and tended greatly to the defeat of the Bill. I have seen it hung up, printed in gilt letters, framed and glazed, not fifteen years ago, in the club room of a public-house, where a Brunswick Lodge had been accustomed to meet. When this poem was written, the Bill had gone up to the Lords, and had been rejected, 18th May, 1825, by a majority of forty-eight. Messrs Leslie Foster, North, and Brownlow had spoken in the House of Commons against the Bill, Mr. North with considerable ability; it is needless to say, the supposition of their conversion is an instance of rhetorical enhancement *per impossibile*, not an allusion to anything that really happened.—I cannot find that Scarlett took more than a colourable part in the debate.—Dr. Bathurst, Bishop of Norwich, spoke in favour of the Bill, shortly and eloquently.

Paget, Marquis of Anglesey, was Lord Lieutenant of Ireland; he had succeeded to the Marquis of Wellesley, displaced for undue concessions to O'Connell; but in 1829 he committed the same offence, and was dismissed by his old chief, the Duke of Wellington, just before the Duke himself gave way.—The Bishop of Chester. Dr. Blomfield, afterwards Bishop of London, followed Bishop Bathurst in a learned speech, with a good many quotations from Juvenal.—The slip about the heir-*apparent* (which should have been heir-*presumptive*) is repeated in the next piece.

I have the authority of the late Lord Belper for ascribing this piece to Praed. There is no title to it as originally printed.]

"So help me God!" - *Speech of the Duke of York.*
"God help thee, silly one!"—*Poetry of the Anti-Jacobin.*

" My lords, since things at last are come
    To such a situation,
That members of the Church of Rome
    Grow weary of starvation;
Since in the Commons House for once
    Some common sense is seated,
Since Mr. Bankes is called a dunce
    And Mr. Peel defeated;
Since Noble Lords begin to joke
    When Orthodoxy preaches,
And toil profanely to provoke
    Meek prelates to make speeches;
Since Plunket is not deemed a thief;
    Since placemen talk of reason;
Since freedom is not unbelief,
    Nor toleration treason,
Nought but a Godhead, or an ass,
    Can mar this wicked work.
My Lords, this Bill shall never pass,
    So help me God!" said York.

" Though Mr. Leslie Foster winced
    From what he once asserted;

Though Mr. Brownlow is convinced,
　　And Mr. North converted;
Though even country gentlemen
　　Are sick of half their maggots,
And rustics mock the Vicar, when
　　He prates of fiery faggots;
Though Hume and Brougham and twenty more
　　Are swaggering and swearing,
And Scarlett hopes the scarlet whore
　　Will not be found past bearing;
Though Reverend Norwich does not mind
　　The feuds of two and seven,
And trusts that humble prayer may find
　　A dozen roads to Heaven;
Till royal heads are lit with gas—
　　Till Hebrews dine off pork—
My Lords, this Bill shall never pass,
　　So help me God!" said York.

" Let England from her slumbers wake
　　To greet her best adviser,
And know, that nought on earth can make
　　The Heir Apparent wiser.
I care not how the seasons fly;
　　How circumstances alter;
I care not for necessity,
　　Which makes Olympus falter;

I care not for a Parliament;
    I care not for a people;
I care not for an argument
    As long as Strasburg steeple;
I care not who are faithful still,
    I care not who are failers,
In short, I care for Burdett's bill
    As much as for my tailor's;
And though the rebels rise *en masse*
    With bludgeon and with fork,
My Lords, this Bill shall never pass,
    So help me God!" said York.

" Oh, yes, let English wrath appal
    The Irish brutes and Catos;
And let the curse of famine fall
    On all who eat potatoes;
Let gold, my Lords, be spent like dust,
    Let blood be spilt like water,
Let churchmen preach by cut and thrust,
    And educate by slaughter;
Let Bradley King and Harcourt Lees
    Awake their zeal and learning,
And nib their pen for rhapsodies,
    And light their torch for burning;
Let Paget choose a proper stand
    Against the Pope's invaders,

And Chester raise his reverend hand
  To bless the Lord's crusaders;
Let Ireland read a mournful mass
  From Holyhead to Cork:
My Lords, this Bill shall never pass,
  So help me God!" said York.

"And think, my Lords! when kings are crowned
  A solemn oath is plighted;
Which he who thinks an empty sound
  Is grievously benighted;
And sure, my Lords, that noble lord
  Has very little breeding
Who asks a king to break his word
  To save a little bleeding!
I speak my own peculiar creed;
  I answer for no other;
Of course I don't presume to read
  The conscience of my brother;
But I, where'er my head may rest,
  Whate'er my lot or station—
I pledge myself to do my best
  To plague the Irish nation.
There once a clever fable was
  About a Log, and Stork:
My Lords, this Bill shall never pass,
  So help me God!" said York.

X.

THE LAY OF THE CHEESE.

[The incident commemorated in this Lay is no fiction. A Cheshire cheese, of 160 lbs. weight, was subscribed for by sundry ardent Protestants residing in Chester, and solemnly presented to the Duke of York, with an enthusiastic address, by the two county members, Mr. Davis Davenport and Mr. Wilbraham Egerton. The address may be read in the *Times* of June 4, 1825, and the Duke's answer, appreciative, but rather short, a few days later. A second cheese was intended for the Diocesan, whose editions of Greek plays of Æschylus had been sharply criticised in the *Edinburgh Review*. History does not say if it was presented.—Lord Eldon writes, about this date, "The Duke of York is at Newmarket. It is to be regretted that, in his highly important and lofty situation, he spends so many days with blacklegs, and so many nights at cards." He had recently been compelled by his creditors to sell Oatlands Park; not before his relations with neighbouring tradesmen had become a scandal, which is still remembered on the spot. —The "lawyer" is probably Lord Eldon, who got the credit, undeservedly, of having put up the Duke to speak the speech.]

"Does your Honour like cheese?" "Like it!" said the Duke, whose good-nature anticipated what was to follow, "cakes and cheese are a dinner for an Emperor!"—*Heart of Midlothian.*

The Pope, that pagan full of pride,
   From whom may Heaven defend us,
Did lay one summer eventide,
   A horrid plot to end us;

O'Connell came and talked his fill ;
Sir Francis Burdett made a Bill ;
And honest men felt great alarms,
Both for their faiths and for their farms,
    Solid men of Cheshire !

We heard around the savage cries
 Of men with ragged breeches,
Who practised the barbarities
 Of making hay—and speeches ;
And Popish priests, disguised like Whigs,
Prepared to steal the Parson's pigs,
To overthrow the Church and steeple
And break the backs of upright people,
    Solid men of Cheshire !

Then up the Heir Apparent got
 Of Britain's wide dominion,
And said that Heaven and Earth should not
 Demolish his opinion ;
That Heirs Apparent were not meant
To listen to an argument,
And bringing Royal Dukes to reason,
He thought, was little short of treason—
    Solid men of Cheshire.

And what reward did men devise
 For such a peroration,

THE LAY OF THE CHEESE. 43

Which saved their lives and liberties
    From transubstantiation?
A long address, filled full of beauties,
Expressive of their loves and duties;
And also a prodigious cheese,
As heavy as Sir Harcourt Lees—
             Solid men of Cheshire.

Rank makes a virtue of a sin;
    Small labour it would cost one
To prove that Peers a cheese may win,
    As Æsop's magpie lost one.
The Prince and pie perhaps inherit
A voice of nearly equal merit;
A fox induced the bird to puke;
A lawyer bammed the Royal Duke—
             Solid men of Cheshire.

"Blest cheese," said girls in grogram vests,
    "Rub off your rural shyness;
And feast his Royal Highness' guests,
    And feast his Royal Highness.
'Tis thine to catch the sweets that slip
From Mr. Peel's melodious lip,
The Chancellor's Bœotian thunders,
And Blomfield's Æschylean blunders—
             Solid men of Cheshire.

"The Parmesan upon the board
   Shall tasteless seem before thee,
And many a spiritual lord
   Shall breathe a blessing o'er thee;
A hallowed spot the shrine shall be,
Where'er a shrine is made for thee,
And none but Reverend Rats shall dare
To taste a single morsel there—
              Solid men of Cheshire."

Alas, the fatal sisters frowned
   Upon the promised pleasure;
The creditors came darkly round,
   And seized the ponderous treasure!
But yet, to ease the Duke's distress,
They forwarded the long address,
Because—to strip the fact of feigning—
The paper was not worth detaining!
              Solid men of Cheshire!

XI.
ROYAL EDUCATION.

A NURSERY SONG.

[A Bill was carried through Parliament in the session of 1826 to give the Duke of Cumberland, the most unpopular member of the Royal Family, £6,000 a year for life, in addition to his other appointments, in consideration of his undertaking to " educate " his son, afterwards the blind King of Hanover; the same who, but for the intervention of the little girl his cousin, would have been one day king of England.—The blank in stanza six must probably be filled with the name of Hook ; see No. V.—The old joke about the Brunswick Royal Family may be recalled—" This Family is the cheapest to see, and dearest to keep, ever known in England."—The poem appeared in the *Morning Chronicle* of 6th July, 1825, signed Φ, and was at the time ascertained to be Praed's by Sir Edward Bunbury, to whom I am indebted for the information.]

I AM a babe of royalty;
Queen Charlotte was my grannam;
And Parliament has voted me
    Six thousand pounds per annum;
To teach me how to read and write,
    To teach me elocution,
To teach me how to feast and fight
    For the king and constitution,

As a well-taught Prince should do,
Who is taught by contribution.

I'll have a doll of porphyry
  With diamonds in her curls,
And a rocking-horse of ivory,
  And a skipping rope of pearls;
I'll have a painted paper kite
  With banker's bills for wings,
And a golden fiddle to play at night
  With a silver wire for strings,
    As a well-taught Prince should have,
    Who is sprung from the German kings.

My woman of the bed chamber
  Shall dress in the finest silk;
And a nobleman of Hanover
  Shall boil my bread and milk;
My breeches shall be of cloth of gold,
  My night-cap of Mechlin lace,
And Cologne water, hot and cold,
  Shall be ready to wash my face,
    As a well-taught Prince should wash,
    Who is come of a royal race.

And when my coach and six shall jog,
  With horns, huzzas, and banners,
To some gaunt German pedagogue
  Who teaches Greek and manners,

ROYAL EDUCATION.

How very ready I shall be
 To show that I'm fit for ruling,
By gaming and by gallantry,
 And other kinds of fooling
  Which a well-taught Prince should learn,
 Who costs so much in schooling.

I'll learn of Uncle George to make
 A sword-knot, and a bow,
And I'll learn of Uncle York to take
 The long odds, and a vow;
And Uncle Clarence shall supply
 The science of imprecation,
And you, my own papa, shall try
 To teach me fabrication,
  Which a well-taught Prince should study,
 Whose tutors are paid by the nation.

I'll learn of Peel his lunacy
 About the priests and popes;
From . . . to live in infamy,
 From Canning to talk in tropes;
From Blomfield to discern new lights,
 To darken the old, from Scott,
From Liverpool the chartered rights
 Which an Englishman has not,
  As a well-taught Prince should know,
 Who is born for a kingly lot.

While education day by day
  My native wit enlarges,
Oh shall I not at last repay
  The country's heavy charges!
As wise as any other Guelph,
  As useful and as dear,
Oh shall I not procure myself
  A people's scorn and fear,
    Which a well-taught Prince should earn,
  With six thousand pounds a year!

XII.
THE CORONATION OF CHARLES X.

I. THE JOURNEY TO RHEIMS.

[In the summer of 1825 Praed was in Paris, travelling with the late Marquis of Ailesbury, then Lord Ernest Bruce, to whom he had acted as private tutor for a short time at Eton. The following poems are evidently the work of an eye-witness; they appeared in the *Morning Chronicle*, 5 and 11 July, 1825. The first has the signature Φ; the second, perhaps through inadvertency, is unsigned.

The accident to the three Dukes really happened. Their horses bolted at a royal salute, and the Duc de Damas, in particular the Minister for Foreign Affairs, afterwards Governor to the Duc de Bordeaux, was seriously hurt.—M. Mazurier, a posture-master, sustained the part of the hero, a baboon called Jocko, in a very French tragedy, in which he saved the baby, and afterwards met the fate of Gelert, being shot dead by mistake.]

"Spectatum veniunt, veniunt spectentur ut ipsi."

Oh was it not a glorious day
For all the mighty nation,
When Charles set out—*le bien aimé*—
To act his coronation!
All people left their old abodes
To aid the celebration,

And purchased flowers, and studied modes,
  In glad anticipation
    Of such a day.

Oh who shall sing the motley hordes
  Of women and of warriors;
Or count the Counts, or laud the Lords,
  Who started from the Barriers!
Canaille was mixed with Cavaliers,
  And fair ones jostled farriers,
And gouty limbs and feeble years
  Cried shame upon the tarriers
    At home that day.

The student started from his books,
  The farmer from his stubble;
The *belle* bestowed upon her looks
  Ten times her usual trouble;
Monsieur for once forgot to swear
  At being made a bubble,
And gaily charged his *tabatière*,
  When *conducteurs* charged double
    Their fare that day.

And there were shouts of deputies
  Awaking from the Session,
And Presidents of Colleges
  To grace the King's procession;

And mayors of little towns came out
  To read their faith's profession,
Which might have been improved, no doubt,
  By half an hour's compression
    The previous day.

The peasants on the journey showed
  Their loyalty was hearty,
By flinging laurels on the road
  Before the Royal Party;
They waved old banners to the skies
  Inscribed "*Non minor Marte*,"
And scratched from their transparencies
  The name of Bonaparté,
    To suit the day.

And right and left upon the way
  They made the cannons rattle;
And babes in arms cried out "*O gai!*
  The French have won a battle!"
And rockets flew about like rain,
  And frightened all the cattle;
Three dukes were very nearly slain,
  Which would have made a tattle
    For many a day.

The king, whose steeds had made a start,
  Composed the fright he woke in,

And gave of his benignant heart
    A most bewitching token:
"*Mon Dieu!*" the gracious monarch said,
    Before the leech had spoken;
"*Mon Dieu!* Has Damas broke his head?
    I wish it had been broken
            Some other day!"

But oh, at Rheims, the day before,
    A hundred prayers were canted,
And dull addresses mumbled o'er,
    And naughty ballads chaunted;
The capital's debauchery
    Was all at once transplanted,
And Etienne *fils* brought *eau de vie*,
    And Vérey's scullion panted
            At Rheims that day.

The cool *Café*, the *cabriolet*,
    Cigars and macaronis,
And *Rouge et noir*, and *eau sucré*,
    And conversaziones;
The loungers of the Tuileries
    Find here their ancient cronies,
And ladies, hot with ecstasies,
    May hurry to Tortoni's
            For ice to-day.

And Father Paul, the Capuchin,
   Is damning all his flock—O!
And pretty little Adeline
   Percurrit pulpita socco;
And rich and poor and peer and boor
   May find at eight o'clock—O!
" *Les premiers soupirs d'Amour* "—
   Les derniers de Jocko—
         Or both, to-day.

So when Apollo from the skies
   Drove down his coach and four—O!
He did not leave one pair of eyes
   Bedewed in Rheims with sorrow;
While those who could not buy a bed,
   And those who could not borrow,
Lay down upon the floor, and said
   " I wish it were to-morrow,
         And not to-day!"

XIII.

THE CORONATION OF CHARLES X.

II.—RHEIMS.

[Marshal Lauriston, an old general of Napoleon, had adhered to the monarchy during the Hundred Days, and held at the Coronation the Court Office of Grand Veneur.—For Moncey, see No. I.—Chateaubriand had just been turned out of the ministry, was turning Liberal, and editing the *Journal des Débats*.—Villéle, the head of the ultra-royalist party, was at this time President of the Council and Minister of Finance.—Percy, Duke of Northumberland, was accredited Ambassador Extraordinary from Great Britain to attend the Coronation; his court suit was said to be worth £75,000. Prince Esterhazy, famous for his jacket of diamonds, held a similar mission on behalf of Austria.—The blue paint, with which the Gothic mouldings of the old Cathedral were bedaubed for this ceremony, is still (1886) to be seen upon them.—Charles X. kept his oath for a little less than five years.]

"Wherefore come ye not to court?
Certain 'tis the rarest sport."—*Skelton.*

"God save the king!"—What God? What king·
In sooth it hardly matters;
For Fortune is a fickle thing,
And as she builds she batters,

The world goes round; the daintiest guest
  May live to gnaw the platters,
And he that wears the purple vest
  May wear the rags and tatters
        Some other day.

An exile looked with signs of grief
  Upon his foreign letters,
And sighed—" Now hang the little thief !
  He bullies all his betters ! "
The dirge is shifted for the dance,
  The creditors are debtors,
The exile reigns in merry France,
  The bully dies in fetters,
        Alas the day !

Rheims ! midwife of French Royalty !
  In thy age-hallowed towers
Reviving Aristocracy
  Sits garlanded with flowers ;
And Order smiles her placid smile
  In spite of Satan's powers,
And sweet Religion all the while
  Rains down benignant showers
        Of Priests to-day. .

But thou didst see another sight
  In that terrific season

When mobs pulled down the matron—Right,
  And crowned the harlot—Reason;
When raving cobblers mended creeds,
  And fishwives babbled treason,
And honest men who told their beads
  Were like to find their weasand
      Cut through some day.

Thou saw'st the painted goddess led
  In triumph through the city;
While monks looked blue and maids looked red
  Before her fierce banditti;
Thou heard'st the drums and trumpets roll,
  When Horror, growing witty,
Made greybeards dance the Carmagnole,
  And virgins sing the ditty
      Of blood that day!

A butcher with unholy feet
  Profaned the shuddering altar;
His surplice was a winding sheet,
  His girdle was a halter.
Alas, where massacre was mass,
  And blasphemy was psalter,
Those hands of iron, throats of brass,
  Did never fail or falter
      At church all day!

Those times are changed. Thy sacred shrine
    Its ancient worship blesses,
And lords and ladies gaily shine
    Amid thy carved recesses;
Long whiskers come, and longer ears,
    False hearts and falser tresses,
Court pages and Court pamphleteers,
    Court follies and Court dresses,
        All new to-day.

There's Marshal Lauriston, quite gay
    In bobbins and in buckles;
And Moncey, who in Spain one day
    Was rapped upon the knuckles;
Chateaubriand, who bawls and broils,
    Villèle, who talks and truckles,
And Talleyrand, who sets the toils,
    And holds his tongue, and chuckles,
        And bides his day.

And Pozzo, whose intruding tread
    Makes such a plaguy racket,
When nations, weary of their Head,
    Lift up a club to crack it;
And Percy's formidable coat,
    And Esterhazy's jacket,

And other clothes of lesser note,
   Sent over by the packet
         To grace the day.

But where's the king? The king's asleep.
   Go, seek our Royal Master,
And tell him that his humble sheep
   Are waiting for their pastor.
The king was sitting in a gown
   As white as alabaster;
"Sire," said the Bishop, with a frown,
   "You should have been much faster
         Asleep to-day!"

And then—the usual farce began,
   And multitudes were staring
To see an old and ugly man
   A velvet night-cap wearing;
The *Moniteur* declares "the whole
   Was solemn beyond bearing;"
And *quantum suff.* of rigmarole,
   And *quantum suff.* of swearing
         Hallowed the day.

He swore to keep his Royal word,
   He swore to keep the Charter,
He swore in no unjust accord
   His creed or Crown to barter;

He swore in all the Church's wars
　To give and take no quarter
He swore to be a modern Mars,
　Or else a modern martyr
　　　　For God some day.

He swore to slay all heresies
　Without the least compunction,
And understand the Trinity's
　Mysterious conjunction;
And having oiled his hands and face
　With Heaven's soul-cleansing unction,
Lay on his belly, full of grace,
　And so obtained the function
　　　　Of KING that day.

" May blessings fall immensely thick
　On him whom Heaven sets o'er us !
And may he be a wall of brick
　Behind us and before us !"
So prayed a paralytic priest
　Most solemn and sonorous ;
The people, anxious for the feast,
　Responded in full chorus
　　　　" Amen !" that day.

Then comes the dinner and the dance,
　And rustic sports and games, Sir ;

And peasants drink the health of France,
And peers dispute for claims, Sir;
And some are calling "*Vive le Roi!*"
And some are calling names, Sir;
And some are calling "*Suivez moi!*"
We've had enough of Rheims, Sir,
For one fine day.

[NOTE.—Sir Francis Burdett's Catholic Relief Bill was rejected in the House of Lords, May 18th, 1825. On the 15th July, the *Morning Chronicle* contained, under the title "No Popery," a copy of verses which I have authority for attributing to Praed. He did not, however, affix any signature to them; and the tone is somewhat shrill for republication. The last two stanzas—the best of ten—will serve for a specimen:—

> Mother Church with joy is unruly
> My Lords the Bishops are dancing a reel;
> Lead out your partners, holy Howley,
> Hair-on-end Lethbridge, and red-headed Peel!
>
> Loud chime the bells of each orthodox steeple
> Mitred palaces, hoist your flags
> And let a chorus of tithe-eating people
> Sing to the praise and glory of Bags!"

"Old Bags," I grieve to say, was a synonym for the Chancellor, who thus notices the event in his correspondence; "The Commons stared me very impudently in the face;... This Bill, however, I think those gentlemen will never see again."—Dr. Howley was then Bishop of London; after this, it was a small matter to tax the Home Secretary with "carrots!"]

XIV.

THE LONDON UNIVERSITY.

A DISCOURSE DELIVERED BY A COLLEGE TUTOR AT A
SUPPER-PARTY.

[Appeared in the *Morning Chronicle* of July 19th, 1825. By the
"London University," it is necessary to explain, was by no means
intended the present anomalous body, which sets papers, and gives
degrees at Burlington House. That Institution was only founded
twelve years later. The London University which Thomas
Campbell promoted, and which Praed sang, was a very substantial
Academic Body, and a real addition to the educational machinery
of the country; and that it has never, up to this year of grace
1887, succeeded in making itself quite intelligible to the inhabitants of London generally, is due to the unkind way in which it
was changed at nurse. Its very name has been appropriated,
since 1837, by an oddly constituted Board of Examinations, which
never had a professor, or a student, in the world; and itself has
been forced to survive under the appellation of "University College,
London." The opposition of Oxford and Cambridge was largely
responsible for this miscarriage.—Crawford, probably an old doctor
of divinity who was archdeacon of Carmarthen, and long before
a Fellow of Trinity.—Dr. Coplestone, Provost of Oriel, Oxford, was
the most conspicuous personage at this time to be found among
Dons at that University.—Canon Kennedy, Praed's rival in the
lighter walks of scholarship, but far superior to him in solid
attainment, was Senior Classic in 1827, and still survives (1887) as
Professor of Greek.—Sir G. B. Airy, till lately Astronomer Royal,

POLITICAL AND OCCASIONAL POEMS.

was Senior Wrangler in 1823.—" New futures from Monckius" is explained by the author himself in a note as follows—" In one of Dr. Monck's learned editions of Greek Plays, a slip of the pen had left a Latin note commencing *Facile* PERSENTIBUNT *juvenes* etc. A caricature of the learned professor appeared soon after on King's Parade, with the inscription as above." Plate-money, a contribution formerly exacted at College from young men of family and fortune, who entered as Fellow-commoners. The ostensible purpose of it was the replenishing of the College plate.— The great meeting at the London Tavern, at which the project of a London University was started, was held 1st July, 1825. The Lord Mayor presided. Speeches were made by Brougham, Russell, Mackintosh, Denman, and Campbell; the last called attention to the fact that London, Constantinople and Madrid were the only European capitals which were without a University; which he defined as "a great place of liberal education, established on a system of combination and cheapness." In that sense London still remains "linked in unholy alliance with the capitals of the Turk and Spaniard." It has been left for the present generation to remove this reproach.]

YE Dons and ye doctors, ye Provosts and Proctors,
  Who are paid to monopolize knowledge,
Come make opposition by voice and petition
  To the radical infidel College;
Come put forth your powers in aid of the towers
  Which boast of their Bishops and Martyrs,
And arm all the terrors of privileged errors
  Which live by the wax of their Charters.

Let Mackintosh battle with Canning and Vattel,
  Let Brougham be a friend to the " niggers,"

Burdett cure the nation's misrepresentations,
    And Hume cut a figure in figures;
But let them not babble of Greek to the rabble,
    Nor teach the mechanics their letters;
The labouring classes were born to be asses,
    And not to be aping their betters.

'Tis a terrible crisis for Cam and for Isis!
    Fat butchers are learning dissection;
And looking-glass-makers become sabbath-breakers
    To study the rules of reflection;
" $\sin : \phi$ " and " $\sin : \theta$ "—what sins can be sweeter?
    Are taught to the poor of both sexes,
And weavers and spinners jump up from their dinners
    To flirt with their Y's and their X's.

Chuckfarthing advances the doctrine of chances
    In spite of the staff of the beadle;
And menders of breeches between the long stitches
    Write books on the laws of the needle;
And chandlers all chatter of luminous matter,
    Who communicate none to their tallows,
And rogues get a notion of the pendulum's motion
    Which is only of use at the gallows.

The impurest of attics read pure mathematics,
    The ginshops are turned into cloisters,

A Crawford next summer will fill you your rummer,
    A Coplestone open your oysters.
The bells of Old Bailey are practising gaily
    The erudite tones of St. Mary's;
The Minories any day will rear you a Kennedy,
    And Bishopsgate blossom with Airys.

The nature of granites, the tricks of the planets,
    The forces of steams and of gases,
The engines mechanical, the long words botanical,
    The ranging of beetles in classes,
The delicate junctions of symbols and functions,
    The impossible roots of equations—
Are these proper questions for Cockney digestions,
    Fit food for a cit's lucubrations?

The eloquent pages of time-hallowed sages
    Embalmed by some critical German,
Old presents from Brunckius, new futures from Monckius,
    The squabbles of Porson with Hermann,
Your Alphas and Betas, your Canons of Metres,
    Your Infinite Powers of Particles,
Shall these and such-like work make journeymen strike work
    And 'prentices tear up their articles?

But oh! since fair Science will cruelly fly hence
    To smile upon vagrants and gipsies,

Since knights of the hammer must handle their
   grammar,
And nightmen account for eclipses,
Our handicraft neighbours shall share in our labours
   If they leave us the whole of the honey,
And the *sans-culotte* caitiff shall start for the plate, if
   He puts in no claim to *plate-money*.

Ye Halls, on whose dais the Don of to-day is
   To feed on the beef and the benison,
Ye Common-room glories, where beneficed Tories
   Digest their belief and their venison,
Ye duels scholastic, where quibbles monastic
   Are asserted with none to confute them,
Ye grave Congregations, where frequent taxations
   Are settled with none to dispute them—

Far hence be the season when Radical treason
   Of port and of pudding shall bilk ye,
When the weavers aforesaid shall taste of our boar's
   head,
The silk-winders swallow our *silky*,
When the mob shall eat faster than any Vice-
   master,
The watermen try to out-tope us,
When Campbell shall dish up a bowl of our
   bishop,
Or Brougham and Co. cope with our *copus*.

XV.

AN EPITAPH ON THE LATE KING OF THE SANDWICH ISLANDS.

BY CRAZEE RATTEE, ESQ., HIS MAJESTY'S POET LAUREATE.

[From the *Morning Chronicle* of 3rd August, 1825, signed Φ, and the last of the series that appeared in its columns. This capital piece was oddly censured by the American Editor of Praed's Poems, as violating the wholesome rule *De mortuis*, etc.; but, it is needless to remark, in 1825 George IV. was alive, and likely to live. The expediency of letting satirists alone had come to be more thoroughly appreciated, since

for showing truth to flattered state
Kind Hunt was shut in prison—

But these verses, as printed, were probably as much as could be dared; and there is a tradition, noticed in *Notes and Queries* for 20th February, 1869, that one stanza was suppressed, of which only the first quatrain has survived

"A noble, nasty race he ran,
Superbly filthy and fastidious;
He was the world's first gentleman,
And made the appellation hideous."

Contrary to his usual practice, Praed wrote three notes on this piece; the first on stanza 7: "In the Sandwich Islands no greater mark of respect can be paid to the parent, by the son, than the swallowing of a part of his mortal remains; more civilized nations are content with the prejudices."—Stanza 9: "When a native of the Sandwich Islands is weary of his first spouse, he may bring home another, but he may not divorce his originally chosen consort."—Stanza 12: "When the Sovereign of the Sandwich Islands dies, each of his subjects shows his respect for the deceased Prince, by extracting a valuable tooth from his head."]

BENEATH the marble, mud, or moss,
    Whiche'er his subjects shall determine,
Entombed in eulogies and dross,
    The Island King is food for vermin.
Preserved by scribblers and by salt
    From Lethe and sepulchral vapours,
His body fills his father's vault,
    His character the daily papers.

Well was he framed for royal seat;
    Kind—to the meanest of his creatures,
With tender heart and tender feet,
    And open purse and open features;
The ladies say who laid him out,
    And earned thereby the usual pensions,
They never wreathed a shroud about
    A corpse of more genteel dimensions.

He warred with half-a-score of foes,
    And shone—by proxy—in the quarrel;
Enjoyed hard fights and soft repose,
    And deathless debt, and deathless laurel;

His enemies were scalped and flayed
    Whene'er his subjects were victorious,
And widows wept, and paupers paid,
    To make their Sovereign ruler glorious.

And days were set apart for thanks,
    And prayers were said by pious readers,
And laud was lavished on the ranks,
    And laurel lavished on their leaders.
Events are writ by History's pen,
    Though causes are too much to care for ;
Fame talks about the where and when,
    While Folly asks the why and wherefore.

In peace he was intensely gay,
    And indefatigably busy,
Preparing gewgaws every day,
    And shows, to make his subjects dizzy ;
And hearing the report of guns,
    And signing the report of gaolers,
And making up receipts for buns
    And patterns for the army tailors,

And building carriages and boats
    And streets and chapels and pavilions,
And regulating all the coats
    And all the principles of millions,

And drinking homilies and gin,
   And chewing pork and adulation,
And looking backwards upon sin,
   And looking forwards to salvation.

The people, in his happy reign,
   Were blest beyond all other nations :
Unharmed by foreign axe or chain,
   Unhealed by civil innovations ;
They served the usual logs and stones
   With all the usual rites and terrors,
And swallowed all their father's bones,
   And swallowed all their father's errors,

When the fierce mob, with clubs and knives,
   All swore that nothing should prevent them,
But that their representatives
   Should actually represent them,
He interposed the proper checks,
   By sending troops, with drums and banners,
To cut their speeches short, and necks,
   And break their heads, to mend their manners.

And when Dissension flung her stain
   Upon the light of Hymen's altar,
And Destiny made Hymen's chain
   As galling as the hangman's halter,

He passed a most domestic life,
  By many mistresses befriended,
And did not put away his wife,
  For fear the priest should be offended.

And thus at last he sank to rest
  Amid the blessings of his people,
And sighs were heard from every heart,
  And bells were tolled from every steeple;
And loud was every public throng
  His public character adorning,
And poets raised a mourning song,
  And clothiers raised the price of mourning.

His funeral was very grand,
  Followed by many robes and maces,
And all the great ones of the land
  Struggling as heretofore, for places;
And every loyal Minister
  Was there, with signs of purse-felt sorrow,
Save Pozzy, his lord-chancellor,
  Who promised to attend " to-morrow."

Peace to his dust. His fostering care
  By grateful hearts shall long be cherished;
And all his subjects shall declare
  They lost a grinder when he perished.

They who shall look upon the lead
    Wherein a people's love hath shrined him,
Will say—when all the worst is said,
    Perhaps he leaves a worse behind him!

XVI.

THE CHAUNTS OF THE BRAZEN HEAD. I.

[The *Brazen Head*, as Charles Knight records in his Autobiography, was a periodical started by him to amuse the Town, during the depression that followed on the commercial crisis of 1826. It failed, though Praed wrote some of his best pieces in it ; and the reason will probably be evident enough to those who refer to its dingy, crowded, and mean-looking pages. Knight's good will as an Editor was greater than his enterprize as a publisher.—This poem reflects the spirit, or decline of spirit, which characterized party politics in the later days of Lord Liverpool's ministers, and of Tory domination.—The ninth stanza is somewhat obscure ; I would paraphrase it : "thanks to the administration of Lord Anglesey in Ireland, and his suppression of the Catholic Association, and thanks to Bishop Blomfield's learned oration, among others, in the Lords, the Anti-Catholics, headed by Wellington and other heroes of the French war, Marshal Beresford for example, and Lord Anglesey himself, have been victorious, and Sir F. Burdett's Catholic Relief Bill has been defeated."—The undue space occupied in this controversy by references to the days of Queen Mary, and to the statute *De Heretico Comburendo*, may be illustrated by Canning's famous lines (1824), printed by Hayward—

> " Yes, Deans shall burn ; and at the funeral pyre,
> With eyes averted from the unhallowed fire—
> Irreverent posture—Harrowby shall stand,
> And hold his coat-tails up with either hand."

See also Macaulay's political squib, the "Country Clergyman's Trip to Cambridge" (1827)—

"How burning would soon come in fashion,
 And how very bad it must feel!"]

"Brazen companion of my solitary hours! do you, while I recline, pronounce a prologue to those sentiments of wisdom and virtue, which are hereafter to be the oracles of statesmen, and the guides of philosophers. Give me to-night a proem of our essay—an opening of our case—a division of our subject. Speak!" (*Slow music. The Friar falls asleep. The Head chaunts as follows.*)—THE BRAZEN HEAD.

I THINK, whatever mortals crave
　With impotent endeavour—
A wreath—a rank—a throne—a grave,
　The world goes round for ever:
I think that life is not too long;
　And therefore I determine,
That many people read a song
　Who will not read a sermon.

I think you've looked through many hearts,
　And mused on many actions,
And studied Man's component parts,
　And Nature's compound fractions:
I think you've picked up truth by bits
　From foreigner and neighbour:
I think the world has lost its wits,
　And you have lost your labour,

I think the studies of the wise,
　The hero's noisy quarrel,

The majesty of Woman's eyes,
    The poet's cherished laurel,
And all that makes us lean or fat,
    And all that charms or troubles—
This bubble is more bright than that,
    But still, they all are bubbles.

I think the thing you call Renown,
    The unsubstantial vapour
For which the soldier burns a town,
    The sonneteer a taper,
Is like the mist which, as he flies,
    The horseman leaves behind him ;
He cannot mark its wreaths arise,
    Or if he does, they blind him.

I think one nod of Mistress Chance
    Makes creditors of debtors,
And shifts the funeral for the dance,
    The sceptre for the fetters :
I think that Fortune's favoured guest
    May live to gnaw the platters,
And he that wears the purple vest
    May wear the rags and tatters.

I think the Tories love to buy
    " Your Lordship "s and " Your Grace "s,

By loathing common honesty,
    And lauding common-places:
I think that some are very wise,
    And some are very funny,
And some grow rich by telling lies,
    And some by telling money.

I think the Whigs are wicked knaves—
    And very like the Tories—
Who doubt that Britain rules the waves,
    And ask the price of glories;
I think that many fret and fume
    At what their friends are planning,
And Mr. Hume hates Mr. Brougham
    As much as Mr. Canning.

I think that friars and their hoods,
    Their doctrines and their maggots,
Have lighted up too many feuds,
    And far too many faggots:
I think, while zealots fast and frown,
    And fight for two or seven,
That there are fifty roads to town,
    And rather more to Heaven.

I think that, thanks to Paget's lance,
    And thanks to Chester's learning,

The hearts that burnt for fame in France
    At home are safe from burning;
I think the Pope is on his back,
    And though 'tis fun to shake him,
I think the Devil not so black
    As many people make him.

I think that Love is like a play
    Where tears and smiles are blended,
Or like a faithless April day
    Where shine with shower is ended;
Like Colnbrook pavement, rather rough,
    Like trade, exposed to losses,
And like a Highland plaid—all stuff,
    And very full of crosses.

I think the world, though dark it be,
    Has aye one rapturous pleasure
Concealed in life's monotony
    For those who seek the treasure;
One planet in a starless night,
    One blossom on a briar,
One friend not quite a hypocrite,
    One woman not a liar!

I think poor beggars court St. Giles,
    Rich beggars court St. Stephen:

And Death looks down with nods and smiles
  And makes the odds all even;
I think some die upon the field,
  And some upon the billow;
And some are laid beneath a shield,
  And some beneath a willow.

I think that very few have sighed
  When fate at last has found them,
Though bitter foes were by their side,
  And barren moss around them.
I think that some have died of drought,
  And some have died of drinking:
I think that nought is worth a thought—
  And I'm a fool for thinking.

XVII.

THE CHAUNTS OF THE BRAZEN HEAD. II.

[The plan of the Magazine, as designed by Charles Knight, was to be the old device of a club of talkers, in the style of the *Noctes Ambrosianæ*, with political interludes from the Head. One of the personages appeals to the oracle to prompt him with the longest odds that can be devised.—Sugden, afterwards Lord St. Leonards, was at this time leader of the Chancery Bar.—Of the theatrical persons mentioned, Mademoiselle Brocard was dancing the principal part in D'Egville's ballets.—For Weber's Oberon see No. VI. The promotion of poor Weber from the worse to the better side of the comparison, between the date of this poem and that of No. VI., may be partly ascribed to his death during the interval.—Brougham charged Canning with "tergiversation," in his place in Parliament. Canning rose, " pale as death," as I have heard the late Mr. Milnes Gaskell describe the scene, "and just said, 'That is a —LIE'—and dropped back on his seat." The usual challenge did not follow.—P. Burmann edited Virgil and other Latin poets.—Mr. Nash, who was a landscape gardener by training, had recently designed the Regent Street fronts; the variety of which is certainly pleasing, though they want dignity.]

BET half the British Parliament
To twice the British Forum ;
Or Sugden's lengthy argument
To Brocard's scant decorum ;

Or Mori's most astounding art
　To Robin's rustic tabor ;
Or twenty bars from old Mozart
　To twenty scores from Weber.

Bet giants' clubs to kitchen brooms,
　Or swords to kitchen pokers,
Or Canning's wit to Mr. Hume's,
　Or Scott's to Mr. Croker's ;
Or Laura's smile, so bright and gay,
　To ocean's richest jewel,
Or Brougham's desire of place and pay
　To Brougham's desire of duel.

Bet honest Wisdom's lightest thought
　To Folly's deepest knowledge ;
Or what is proper to be taught
　To what is taught—at college ;
Or rotten eggs to rotten votes,
　Or Englishmen to Germans,
Or half-a-dozen of Wentworth's notes
　To half a quire of Burmann's.

Bet turtle-soup to vulgar tripe,
　Or Regent Street to Holborn

Or puffs from a tobacco-pipe
　　To puffs from Mr. Colburn ;
Or venison to a crust of bread,
　　Or perigords to fritters,
Or Friar Bacon's Brazen Head
　　To all the gold that glitters.

XVIII.

THE CHAUNTS OF THE BRAZEN HEAD. III.

[The *Brazen Head* expired 10th May, 1826. The next year produced plenty of novelty in politics; the exit of Lord Liverpool; the resignation of Lord Eldon; the Liberal Ministry of Canning, his strangely unequal struggle against the old Tories, and the old Whigs; his death, and the rapid ripening of the Catholic Question, and of the Reform movement. But nothing of all this was evident twelve months before.—Madame Vestris had recently been playing Rosalind, and Apollo in *Midas*.]

THE world pursues the very track
   Which it pursued at its creation;
And mortals shrink in horror back
   From any hint of innovation;
From year to year the children do
   Exactly what their sires have done;
TIME IS—TIME WAS—there's nothing new—
   There's nothing new beneath the sun!

Still lovers hope to be believed,
   Still clients hope to win their causes;
Still plays and farces are received
   With most encouraging applauses;

Still dancers have fantastic toes,
   Still dandies shudder at a dun;
Still diners have their fricandeaus—
   There's nothing new beneath the sun.

Still cooks torment the hapless eels,
   Still boys torment the dumb cockchafers;
Lord Eldon still adores the seals,
   Lord Clifford still adores the wafers;
Still asses have enormous ears,
   Still gambling bets are lost and won;
Still opera dancers marry peers—
   There's nothing new beneath the sun.

Still women are absurdly weak,
   Still infants dote upon a rattle;
Still Mr. Martin cannot speak
   Of anything but beaten cattle;
Still brokers swear the shares will rise,
   Still Cockneys boast of Manton's gun;
Still listeners swallow monstrous lies—
   There's nothing new beneath the sun.

Still genius is a jest to Earls,
   Still honesty is down to zero;
Still heroines have spontaneous curls,
   Still novels have a handsome hero;

Still Madame Vestris plays a man,
    Still fools adore her—I for one;
Still youths write sonnets to a fan—
    There's nothing new beneath the sun.

Still people make a plaguy fuss
    About all things that don't concern them,
As if it matters aught to us
    What happens to our grandsons, burn them!
Still life is nothing to the dead;
    Still Folly's toil is Wisdom's fun;
And still, except the Brazen Head,
    There's nothing new beneath the sun.

XIX.
UTOPIA.

[No apology is necessary for including this piece, apparently a favourite with the author, in this collection; although it has already appeared in the collected Poems. I have substituted it for "A Chapter of Ifs," which seems to me not to be, except perhaps in part, by Praed.—Best, Chief Justice of the Common Pleas, afterwards Lord Wynford, in his then recent judgment in the case of *Fisher v. Stockdale*, laid down very strongly the doctrine that a libel, the truth of which is not proved in a civil action, must be taken to be, not only scandalous, but false. This position, taken in conjunction with the older doctrine "the greater the truth the greater the libel," leads to a curious logical dilemma. The poet does not seem to mean exactly what the Chief Justice meant.— The *Morning Post*, till Praed himself took it in hand in 1832, was a very inferior newspaper. See Macaulay's Essay on Croker's Boswell, and "The Theatrical Alarm-bell," in the *Rejected Addresses*—For the *John Bull* see No. V.—There were two members of the Bankes family at this time in Parliament; Henry, the father, and George, the son; William Henry, the other son, had been defeated in 1825 for Cambridge University by Lord Palmerston.— Lord Eldon's proffered resignations were many; but it may safely be said he was never sorry when they were refused; he resigned, however, effectually, after an adverse vote or two in the House of Commons, on the formation of Canning's Ministry. This instalment of Utopia was realised in April 1827, the same month in which the poem appeared, in the pages of the *New Monthly Magazine*.—Wellesley Pole, a nephew of the Duke of Wellington, was

UTOPIA.

the most notable spendthrift of his day, and behaved, moreover, very badly to his wife.—Mr. Bochsa was a ballet-master, of worse than indifferent reputation.]

———" I can dream, sir,
If I eat well and sleep well."—THE MAD LOVER.

IF I could scare the light away,
 No sun should ever shine ;
If I could bid the clouds obey,
 Thick darkness should be mine ;
Where'er my weary footsteps roam,
 I hate whate'er I see ;
And Fancy builds a fairer home
 In Slumber's hour for me.

I had a vision yesternight
 Of a lovelier land than this,
Where heaven was clothed in warmth and light,
 Where earth was full of bliss ;
And every tree was rich with fruits,
 And every field with flowers,
And every zephyr wakened lutes
 In passion-haunted bowers.

I clambered up a lofty rock
 And did not find it steep ;
I read through a page and a-half of Locke
 And did not fall asleep ;

I said whate'er I may but feel,
  I paid whate'er I owe,
And I danced one day an Irish reel
  With the gout in every toe.

And I was more than six feet high,
  And fortunate, and wise;
And I had a voice of melody
  And beautiful black eyes;
My horses like the lightning went,
  My barrels carried true,
And I held my tongue at an argument,
  And winning cards at loo.

I saw an old Italian priest
  Who spoke without disguise;
I dined with a judge who swore, like Best,
  All libels should be lies;
I bought for a penny a two-penny loaf
  Of wheat—and nothing more;
I danced with a female *philosophe*
  Who was not quite a bore.

The kitchens there had richer roast,
  The sheep wore whiter wool;
I read a witty *Morning Post*,
  And an innocent *John Bull;*

The gaolers had nothing at all to do,
　The hangmen looked forlorn,
And the Peers had passed a vote or two
　For freedom of trade in corn.

There was a crop of wheat, which grew
　Where plough was never brought;
There was a noble Lord, who knew
　What he was never taught;
A scheme appeared in the *Gazette*
　For a lottery without blanks;
And a Parliament had lately met
　Without a single Bankes.

And there were kings who never went
　To cuffs for half-a-crown;
And lawyers who were eloquent
　Without a wig and gown;
And sportsmen who forebore to praise
　Their greyhounds and their guns,
And poets who deserved the bays,
　And did not dread the duns.

And boroughs were bought without a test,
　And no man feared the Pope,
And the Irish cabins were all possest
　Of liberty, and soap;

And the Chancellor, feeling very sick,
   Had just resigned the seals ;
And a clever little Catholic
   Was hearing Scotch Appeals.

I went one day to a court of law
   Where a fee had been refused ;
And a public school I really saw
   Where the rod was never used :
And the sugar still was very sweet,
   Though all the slaves were free ;
And all the folk in Downing Street
   Had learnt the Rule of Three.

There love had never a fear or doubt ;
   December breathed like June ;
The Prima Donna ne'er was out
   Of temper—or of tune ;
The streets were paved with mutton-pies,
   Potatoes ate like pine,
Nothing looked black but woman's eyes,
   Nothing grew old but wine.

There was no fault in the Penal Code,
   No dunce in a public school,
No dust or dirt on a private road,
   No shame in Wellesley Pole.

They showed me a *figurante*, whose name
    Had never known disgrace,
And a gentleman of spotless fame
    With Mr. Bochsa's face.

It was an idle dream; but thou,
    The worshipped one, wert there,
With thy dark clear eyes and beaming brow,
    White neck and floating hair;
And oh, I had an honest heart,
    And a house of Portland stone;
And thou wert dear—as still thou art;
    And more than dear—my own!

Oh bitterness! The morning broke
    Alike on boor and bard;
And thou wert married when I woke
    And all the rest was marred;
And toil and trouble, noise and steam,
    Came back with the coming ray;
And, if I thought the dead could dream,
    I'd hang myself to-day!

XX.

THE DEATH OF CANNING.

[This is the piece to which Charles Knight alludes (Passages of a Working Life, Vol. ii., p. 52), as having been "altered, in his own obtuse fashion" by Mr. James Silk Buckingham, in the columns of his paper, the *Sphynx*. It was written, as Knight informed me. one evening, when a few friends met together had been remarking with bitterness upon the want of concern exhibited by the newspapers at Canning's death. One of the party said to Praed "Why don't you write something?" whereupon he retired to a side-table, and produced these lines. Knight seized upon them at once for his paper—he was sub-editing for Buckingham at the time—and they appeared accordingly, 12th August, 1827, in that shortlived periodical, the precursor of the *Athenæum*, over the signature Φ. The "alterations" made by Buckingham I cannot trace; and I think it possible Mr. Knight's memory deceived him, since he gave me as authentic a MS. copy, which turns out to be identical with the version in the *Sphynx*. But see note on No. XXII. A fierce attack was made by Lord Grey on Canning's ministry when first formed. It did not prevent Brougham and others, of the younger school of Liberalism, from lending him a much needed support. But it seems to have effectually alienated Praed from Whiggism. Lord Lansdowne excepted, who supported Canning, he has no good word, after this, for any of his old leaders and associates.]

VIII. August MDCCCXXVII.

Ay, mourn to-day! but mourn for those
  Whose rights his arm defended;
Whose foes were his and Freedom's foes
  Where'er the names were blended;

For the serf, whose rest from toil and pain
  His mercy might have spoken;
For the slave, whose cold and galling chain
  His vengeance might have broken;

For Helle's stream, where the Pasha's flag
  Still waves o'er the sacred water;
For Erin's huts, where the Orange rag
  Is still the sign of slaughter.

Ay, mourn to-day! but not for him;
  His name is writ in story,
Ere a single cloud could make more dim
  The noon-day of its glory.

Victor in boyhood's early game
  And youth's career of gladness,
Victor in manhood's lists of fame
  O'er envy, hate, and madness,

What could he hope in other years,
  If the longest life had crowned him,
But thus to die, with a nation's tears
  And a world's applause around him?

The laurel wreath upon his brow
  Might have looked less green to-morrow;
But the leaves will bloom for ever now,
  They are newly twined by sorrow.

The sighs that are whispered o'er his clay
  May weary Heaven's Recorder;
But none are glad, save the Turk's Serai,
  And a few of Lord Grey's "Order"!

XXI.
THE RIDDLES OF THE SPHINX.

[There is no reason why Praed should continue to be saddled with Mr. Buckingham's bad spelling of his newspaper's name. This appeared August 19th, 1827, signed Φ.—Canning's death had left the leadership of the country in the hands of the Whigs; but it threw back that of the House of Commons, for a short time, into the hands of the Tories. Reform loomed terribly nearer. The old age was dead, or dying.—Melville, the son of Pitt's Dundas, and his successor in the "management" of Scotland, was driven out, because Canning had no mind to leave so much Parliamentary influence in the hands of an enemy; he was to have been replaced by Lord Binning, "without portfolio."—Lord Bexley, the Vansittart of Lord Liverpool's Exchequer and the "old woman" of Macaulay's "Wellingtoniad," had managed to explain, on May 2nd, that he resigned his office, the Chancellorship of the Duchy of Lancaster, because he had been led to believe that the Catholic Claims would no longer be, under Canning, as they had been under Liverpool, an open question in the Cabinet; but that when he found he was mistaken, he "hastened to retrace the step."—Sir Thomas Lethbridge was put up, May 11th and 18th, to badger Canning with questions in regard to the terms on which anti-Catholic members of the Administration had accepted office, and on which members of the Opposition had promised support. These were sore points with Canning, since the time was yet unripe for a coalition with the Whigs. After giving guarded replies to some of the questions, he refused further information, and challenged a motion.]

'TWAS night; the House was cleared,
  And hushed the fierce debate,
And robed in clouds the Sphinx appeared
  Before St. Stephen's gate.
A virgin's face above,
  A lion's form beneath,
Upon those lips was maiden love,
  Within those claws was death.

She look'd on that high Hall
  With a grim and scornful smile;
And vapours passed like a funeral pall
  O'er Heaven's expanse the while;
And the moon went back that hour
  In an unforetold eclipse,
As the words of mystery and power
  Fell from the marble lips.

" Can ye teach the Owl to meet
  The light of the morning skies?
Can ye make the rays of reason sweet
  To a bigot's blinking eyes?
Can ye bar the lightning's track
  With a canopy of cloth?
Can ye beat a nation's fury back
  With Bibles and cheap broth?

"Can ye count the grains of sand
 On Ocean's stormy beach,
Or the blunders that Lord Westmoreland
 Makes in a single speech?
Can ye read what words are writ
 On the tombs of sacred Nile,
Or construe Mr. Bankes's wit,
 When he makes the gallery smile?

"What drove Lord Melville out?
 What made Lord Bexley stay?
And why does Londonderry spout?
 And why do asses bray?
Why does the morning dawn
 When Phœbus takes his seat?
And why does all the peerage yawn
 When Redesdale talks of wheat?

"How shall the blind discern
 That black is never white?
How shall a rotten borough learn
 That wrong is never right?
How shall fair health be sought
 In the shade of a upas tree,
Or how shall honest deeds be wrought
 In Sarum or Tralee?

"Why does the Earth turn round?
　　And why does the *Morning Post?*
And when will the longitude be found,
　　Or the art of reigning lost?
And when will ice be warm?
　　And when will wrath be cool?
And when will love be not a charm,
　　And a minstrel not a fool?"

While cards were cut in the Hell,
　　And capers on the stage,
While night on the monarch's palace fell,
　　And on the student's page,
The riddling Sphinx thus sung
　　Her how, and when, and why,
And like Sir Thomas, questions flung
　　With none to make reply.

XXII.
THE OUTS.

[Appeared in the *Sphynx*, 16th Sept., 1827.—Although the Ministry formed by Lord Goderich was in no case to live, it would not have been made stronger by re-admitting the Old Guard of Anti-Catholics, whose names are recounted in the first stanza of this poem. The Duke of Wellington, indeed, rejoined it, to Lord Eldon's unspeakable disgust ; and when, a few months later, Lord Goderich's faint heart failed him, he proceeded to " carry on the King's Government," and to tumble from one Liberal measure to another. But the old Outs, the men who were in with Liverpool, and remembered the rule of George the Third—their day was over, for good.—Though Lord Bathurst did not effect much for the advance of our Colonial Empire, he had more Capes, Islands and Harbours named after him than any other man alive, crowned heads only excepted.—Lord Londonderry, brother to the Lord Londonderry who was better known as Castlereagh, and himself better known as the Sir Charles Stuart of the Peninsular war. had by length and distinction of diplomatic service deserved a pension, but was certainly too rich to need it.—The Duke of Newcastle, at the time of the trial of the Queen, was guilty of one of the worst of the many errors which were committed by the King's friends, in declaring his conviction that, having read the evidence, he was as capable of pronouncing a verdict, as if he had not been prevented, by " domestic business of a very pressing character," from being present during the trial.—For Fitzgerald, see the Preface. There are several pieces in the *Morning Post* of this season written in the heroic couplet, but I am not able to identify any of them in particular as Fitzgerald's.—I think this poem, whatever may be the case with No. XX., shows traces of Buckingham's editorship, in the false rhyme of the last stanza. It is signed with a Q., which may perhaps be interpreted as "altered from Φ." I note that Praed's contributions do not appear again in this journal : and that in a laudatory review, dated 1st Dec., 1827, of Knight's Annual, the "Friendship's Offering" for 1828, Buckingham is entirely silent as to Praed's contributions, which are out and out the best things in it. This shows that there had been a quarrel. The signature Q is subsequently affixed to all but the first of a long dull series of "Epistles to Great Public Characters," with which during the few remaining days of the *Sphynx* Praed's defection was in vain attempted to be supplied. The same false rhyme, "bay" and "democracy," turns up in the second of these productions, which I believe to be Buckingham's own.]

    WHEN Eldon can a judgment pass
        In less than half an age,
    When Westmoreland eschews a lass,
        And Melville patronage,
    When Peel forsakes his bigotry
        And gives free thought the rein,
    When Bathurst rears a colony—
        They may come back again.

    When Bexley ceases to be saint,
        And Wetherell to prose,
    When Manners, free of Orange taint,
        Shakes hands with Popish foes,
    When Lethbridge, dropping thoughts of pelf,
        In patriotic vein,
    Can England substitute for self,
        They may come back again.

When Londonderry, matchless peer,
  His pension-hope outlives,
When Newcastle the cause shall hear
  Before he verdict gives,
When Ellenborough's sage replies
  Shall rival Canning's strain,
And beardless Castlereagh grow wise,
  They may come back again.

When Cobbett, guiltless of hard names,
  Pays debts with effort stoic,
And when the *Post* Fitzgerald shames
  In spouting mock heroic;
When Southey, fixed at last in creed,
  Shall other change disdain,
When Lees from Romish fears is freed,
  They may come back again.

When honest men in lawyers thrive,
  And Law knows no delay;
When Tory institutes outlive
  The Chart of Liberty;
When Britons, pining for his rule,
  Import a King from Spain—
The worthy head for such a school,
  They may come back again.

XXIII.

THE RETROSPECT.

[In 1828 Praed appears to have sent two pieces to the *Times* newspaper. This appeared on the 22nd May of that year, unsigned. Sir F. Burdett's Catholic Relief Bill was now passing again through the Commons, and a conference was arranged between the two Houses, which came to nothing.—Praed returns to Lord Eldon:

> Ecce iterum Crispinus, et est mihi sæpe vocandus
> Ad partes, monstrum nulla virtute redemptum.

He was now excluded from office, half estranged from the Ministerial Tories, and seemed to survive only for the purpose of opposing the Liberal movement in politics.—I have no authority, other than that of internal evidence, to justify me in ascribing this piece to Praed; but I do not expect that the ascription will be challenged.]

When Pitt was Premier, well-a-day!
   I chanted *Io Pæans*,
And held the loftiest Whigs at bay
   As well as base plebeians.
I filled old Jacobins with awe,
   Distorting fact and reason,
Whene'er 'twas wished to twist the law
   Or find constructive treason.

I raved at all Republicans,
   Detested snobbish hooters,
Got flattery from partisans,
   And fees from Chancery suitors;
Reform I constantly decried,
   Pronounced the truth a libel,
On working days to briefs applied,
   On Sundays read my Bible.

At length my loyalty was such
   It could but be rewarded;
And, as I ne'er expected much,
   A trifle was accorded.
Content the humble boon I took,
   A coronet and pension,
And on the woolsack proudly shook
   An Earldom's full dimension.

I kept the conscience of the king
   With Protestant discernment;
And showed that freedom was a thing
   Fit only for adjournment;
That granting rights to Catholics
   Would be a dreadful omen,
And millions—say some five or six—
   Were positively no men.

In short, there's nothing more required
    Than bayonets and bullets,
At reasonable prices hired,
    To stop those Irish gullets;
But God forbid I e'er should be
    Like that vile Popish Bonner,
Who *roasted* folks for heresy,
    And for the Church's honour!

I would not burn the wretches—faugh!
    But hanging, drawing, quart'ring
Are quite agreeable to law
    Which disapproves of tort'ring;
And really, if they will persist
    In actions contumacious,
Why then increase the Army List,
    And shoot the most audacious!

But ah, the times are changed! and now,
    Repenting old oppressions,
Majorities are bound to bow
    In favour of concessions;
Yet I will still consistent be,
    Intolerant and Tory,
And go down to posterity
    In pure and perfect glory,

XXIV.
BIGOTRY'S REMONSTRANCE.

[The subject is the same as the last. This will be found in the *Times* of 9th June, 1828, signed P. Its story is pleasantly told in the following extract from a private letter,—written under date July 25th, after a flying visit to Cambridge :
"On the Tuesday following (July 8th) I had a very pleasant party indeed. Ord, as I told you, was taken to Cambridge by Lord Lansdowne. On the road they were speaking of Tom Moore's songs in the *Times* newspaper, and Lord Lansdowne instanced one which he liked particularly. N.B., there was a very tiny compliment to his Lordship in it. Ord was able to tell him that the verses in question were *mine*, as they were written a few weeks before in his chambers; upon which my Lord said a great many civil things of me, and desired Ord to introduce me to him. No opportunity for this ceremony took place at Cambridge, and therefore, upon our return the Ex-Secretary of State (I am sorry for the Ex-) sent to ask me to dinner."

Philpotts, afterwards Bishop of Exeter, was Rector of Stanhope, and a notable pamphleteer against Catholic Emancipation. See note on Lord Kenyon, under No. XXV. "Crocky," *i.e.*, Crockford's, the great gambling house in St. James's St., was just rebuilt and greatly enlarged; it was introduced by Praed in his "Good Night to the Season," the year before, as

"The Hell, where the Fiend in his glory
Sits staring at putty and stones,
And scrambles from story to story
To rattle at midnight his bones."

The sounding phrase "Child and Champion of Jacobinism," here converted to other purposes, is from an invective of Pitt's against Bonaparte, delivered 17th Feb., 1800. This speech was reported by Coleridge for the *Morning Post*, and the merit of its eloquence, including the authorship of this phrase, is claimed by Sara Coleridge for her father (*Essays on his own Times*, p. 1010). —Frederic, Duke of York, died Jan. 1827. Canning's last illness was attributed to the effects of a chill received at his funeral.— Lord King, a clever but feather-headed speaker, of advanced Liberal views, was much in the habit of amusing himself by startling the House of Peers from its propriety; getting sometimes roughly handled in return.]

'Twas dead midnight, when Bigotry came
 With Philpotts for her guide,
And shook her torch of sulphury flame
 At old John Scott's bedside.

"Awake!" she said, "for my soul is sick,
 Our throne is crumbling fast,
And Common Sense the heretic
 Is rending my chain at last.

"Yet Lethbridge is peacefully going to sleep,
 As most of his hearers do,
And Goulburn sits in a reverie deep,
 Dreaming of two times two.

"And dandies are carelessly sipping the froth
 From the Sillery in Pall Mall,
And Crocky is happily laying the cloth
 For the layers of odds in Hell.

"They are blinded all by Priests and Popes,
    They do not pity Peel ;
They have ceased to fear O'Connell's tropes,
    And the metaphors of Sheil.

" Awake, John Scott ; once more advance
    For the Church and Constitution,
The Champion still of Ignorance,
    The Child of Persecution.

" And quail not thou for wrath or scorn ;
    I bring thee arms to-night
Of stouter mould than ever were worn
    By Thetis' son in fight :

" The sword of falsehood, to contend
    That Lansdowne's white is black ;
The shield of dulness strong, to send
    The jests of Holland back :

" Abuse, which seems to the Tory host
    The language of sobriety,
And cant, which sounds to the *Morning Post*
    Like the tone of the truest piety.

" Go feign and flatter, preach and croak,
    Beseech, reprove, upbraid ;

And ever and anon invoke
Thy Frederic's holy shade.

"Tell of the faggots of ancient years
Lit up by Monk and Friar,
Shed, if thou canst, appropriate tears,
And call Lord King a liar.

"Then lull their Lordships to repose
With a quibble or a pun;
There's a proper theme in a nation's woes
For a Merry-Andrew's fun.

"His Majesty shall clasp thy hand
When the hallowed strife is o'er,
And the princely lungs of Cumberland
Shall give thee one cheer more!"

XXV.
TWENTY-EIGHT AND TWENTY-NINE.

[From the *New Monthly Magazine*, January 1829, signed Φ. For O'Connell's "Rent," see No. VIII.—The second Lord Kenyon was a Tory of no note; but he had handed to Philpotts, the pamphleteering clergyman, some private correspondence of George III. with his father, in which the Monarch had sought and received, from Kenyon and Scott, then Lord Chief Justice and Attorney-General respectively, unknown to his Ministers, the fatal advice to trust his own "conscience," in deciding whether Pitt's proposals for relief of the Catholics were, or were not, contrary to his Coronation Oath. Lord Plunket censured this publication in his speech of June 10th, 1828. By praying in aid the conscience of the late king in a matter of state, Lord Kenyon might certainly be said to have aimed at "sinking the nation," somewhat below the surface.—Mathews was at this time performing in his "monodramas" during the season, and acting in the regular drama when winter came.—For Hook, see No. V.—Warren was a manufacturer of boot-blacking, and the inventor of that system of advertising which consists in defacing other people's walls.—General Jackson was elected President of the United States in 1828. His defeat of the English forces at New Orleans in 1814 was a natural subject of glorification to his compatriots.—Corder's murder of his sweetheart, Maria Martin, known as the "Red Barn Murder," was the subject of a ballad which I have heard sung by villagers a generation later. The crime was said to have been discovered through a dream of the victim's mother.—Hugh Blair's sermons had a celebrity which appears unaccountable to a subsequent generation. A collection of the "Sentimental Beauties" in his writings was published in 1809.]

"*Rien n'est changé, mes amis!*"

I HEARD a sick man's dying sigh,
    And an infant's idle laughter;
The Old Year went with mourning by,
    The New came dancing after.
Let Sorrow shed her lonely tear,
    Let Revelry hold her ladle!
Bring boughs of cypress for the bier,
    Fling roses on the cradle!
Mutes to wait on the funeral state!
    Pages to pour the wine!
A requiem for Twenty-eight,
    And a health to Twenty-nine!

Alas for human happiness!
    Alas for human sorrow!
Our yesterday is nothingness—
    What else will be our morrow?
Still Beauty will be stealing hearts
    And Knavery stealing purses;
Still cooks must live by making tarts,
    And wits by making verses:
While sages prate, and courts debate,
    The same stars set and shine;
And the world as it rolled through Twenty-eight
    Must roll through Twenty-nine.

Some king will come, in Heaven's good time,
    To the tomb his father came to;
Some thief will wade through blood and crime
    To a crown he has no claim to;
Some suffering land will rend in twain
    The manacles that bound her,
And gather the links of the broken chain
    To fasten them proudly round her :
The grand and great will love and hate
    And combat and combine ;
And much where we were in Twenty-eight
    We shall be in Twenty-nine.

O'Connell will toil to raise the rent,
    And Kenyon to sink the nation ;
And Sheil will abuse the Parliament,
    And Peel the Association ;
And the thought of bayonets and swords
    Will make ex-Chancellors merry,
And jokes will be cut in the House of Lords,
    And throats in the county Kerry ;
And writers of weight will speculate
    On the Cabinet's design,
And just what it did in Twenty-eight
    It will do in Twenty-nine.

Mathews will be extremely gay,
    And Hook extremely dirty,

And brick and mortar still will say
  "Try Warren—number thirty;"
And General Sauce will have its puff,
  And so will General Jackson,
And peasants will drink up heavy stuff,
  Which they pay a heavy tax on;
And long and late at many a fête
  Gooseberry champagne will shine,
And as old as it was in Twenty-eight
  It will be in Twenty-nine.

John Thomas Mugg, on a lonely hill,
  Will do a deed of mystery;
The *Morning Chronicle* will fill
  Five columns with the history;
The jury will be all surprise,
  The prisoner quite collected,
And Justice Park will wipe his eyes
  And be very much affected;
And folks will relate poor Corder's fate
  As they hurry home to dine,
Comparing the hangings of Twenty-eight
  With the hangings of Twenty-nine.

And the Goddess of Love will keep her smiles,
  And the God of cups his orgies,

And there'll be riots in St. Giles',
    And weddings in St. George's;
And mendicants will sup like kings,
    And lords will swear like lackeys,
And black eyes oft will lead to rings,
    And rings will lead to black eyes;
And pretty Kate will scold her mate,
    In a dialect all divine:
Alas, they married in Twenty-eight,
    They will part in Twenty-nine!

A Curate will go from the house of prayer
    To wrong his worthy neighbour,
By dint of quoting the text of Blair
    And singing the songs of Weber;
Sir Harry will leave the Craven hounds
    To trace the guilty parties,
And ask of the Court five thousand pounds
    To prove how racked his heart is;
And an advocate will execrate
    The spoiler of Hymen's shrine,
And the speech that did for Twenty-eight
    Will do for Twenty-nine.

My uncle will swathe his gouty limbs,
    And talk of his oils and blubbers;

My aunt, Miss Dobbs, will play longer hymns,
    And rather longer rubbers ;
My cousin in Parliament will prove
    How utterly ruined trade is ;
My brother at Eton will fall in love
    With half a hundred ladies ;
My patron will sate his pride from plate,
    And his thirst from the Bordeaux wine ;
His nose was red in Twenty-eight,
    'Twill be redder in Twenty-nine.

And oh ! I shall find how, day by day,
    All thoughts and things look older ;
How the laugh of pleasure grows less gay,
    And the heart of friendship colder ;
But still I shall be what I have been,
    Sworn foe to Lady Reason,
And seldom troubled with the spleen,
    And fond of talking treason ;
I shall buckle my skate, and leap my gate,
    And throw—and write—my line ;
And the woman I worshipped in Twenty-eight
    I shall worship in Twenty-nine.

XXVI.

WATERLOO.

[Appeared in the *Literary Souvenir* for 1831, unsigned ; but I have seen the or.ginal, dated Feb. 1st, 1830. At this time it was the fashion with French writers to assume that the English had already been beaten at Waterloo, when somehow the French got "betrayed." See especially the *Relation* of General Gourgaud, published 1818. In the next generation, Victor Hugo invented the "hollow road of Ohain," to account for the French cavalry *not* "breaking the English squares."]

"On this spot the French cavalry charged, and broke the English squares !"—*Narrative of a French Tourist.*
"Is it true, think you?"—*Winter's Tale.*

Ay, here such valorous deeds were done
    As ne'er were done before ;
Ay, here the reddest wreath was won
    That ever Gallia wore ;
Since Ariosto's wondrous Knight
    Made all the Paynims dance,
There never dawned a day so bright
    As Waterloo's on France.

The trumpet poured its deafening sound,
    Flags fluttered on the gale,

And cannon roared, and heads flew round
  As fast as summer hail;
The sabres flashed their light of fear,
  The steeds began to prance;
The English quaked from front to rear—
  They never quake in France!

The cuirassiers rode in and out
  As fierce as wolves and bears;
'Twas grand to see them slash about
  Among the English squares!
And then the Polish Lancer came
  Careering with his lance;
No wonder Britain blushed for shame,
  And ran away from France!

The Duke of York was killed that day;
  The king was sadly scarred;
Lord Eldon, as he ran away,
  Was taken by the Guard;
Poor Wellington with fifty Blues
  Escaped by some mischance;
Henceforth I think he'll hardly choose
  To show himself in France.

So Buonaparte pitched his tent
  That night in Grosvenor Place,

And Ney rode straight to Parliament
And broke the Speaker's mace;
" *Vive l' Empereur* " was said and sung
From Peebles to Penzance;
The Mayor and Aldermen were hung;
Which made folks laugh in France.

They pulled the Tower of London down;
They burnt our wooden walls;
They brought the Pope himself to town
And lodged him in St. Paul's;
And Gog and Magog rubbed their eyes,
Awaking from a trance,
And grumbled out, in great surprise,
"Oh mercy! we're in France!"

They sent a Regent to our Isle,
The little King of Rome;
And squibs and crackers all the while
Blazed in the Place Vendôme;
And ever since, in arts and power,
They're making great advance;
They've had strong beer from that glad hour,
And sea-coal fires, in France.

My uncle, Captain Flanigan,
Who lost a leg in Spain,

Tells stories of a little man
  Who died at St. Helène;
But bless my heart, they can't be true;
  I'm sure they're all romance;
John Bull was beat at Waterloo!
  They'll swear to that in France.

XXVII.
MARS DISARMED BY LOVE.

[This appeared in the *Gem* of 1831. It was the custom with Editors of Annuals to procure steel engravings from designs by artists of the day, and then ask for poems or stories, from contributors, to illustrate them. Mars and Venus, and Cupid flying away with the sword, were the subject of one of these illustrations, designed by Howard, R.A., and engraved by Warren.—Sir Thomas Sherlock Gooch, of Benacre Hall, often coupled with Sir T. Lethbridge as a stout champion of the Corn Laws, was M.P. for Suffolk for twenty-four years. In the first published draft of " Utopia " Praed has
" a man named Gooch was arguing
For a free trade in corn."

Pitt Club dinners, probably, were responsible for the association of his name with loyal and patriotic toasts.—Don Pedro, who claimed the crown of Portugal for his infant daughter, and Don Miguel, who had usurped it for himself, were still at loggerheads.—The Saxon Prince John, and the Coburg Prince Leopold, had both recently declined the kingdom of Greece, the latter on the ground that there was not enough of Greece to make a kingdom, in default of Epirus and Thessaly.—Turkey was contending unsuccessfully against Russia in Armenia, and apprehending an invasion in the Danubian provinces.—Paris turned out her own Bourbons, and they turned out the Dey of Algiers, both in 1830, and almost simultaneously.]

Ay, bear it hence, thou blessed child;
Though dire the burden be

And hide it in the pathless wild,
   Or drown it in the sea !
The ruthless murderer prays and swears—
   So let him swear and pray !
Be deaf to all his oaths and prayers,
   And take the sword away.

We've had enough of fleets and camps,
   Guns, glories, odes, gazettes,
Triumphal arches, coloured lamps,
   Huzzas and epaulettes;
We could not bear upon our head
   Another leaf of bay;
That horrid Buonaparte's dead;
   Yes, take the sword away.

We're weary of the noisy boasts
   That pleased our patriot throngs;
We've long been dull to Gooch's toasts,
   And deaf to Dibdin's songs;
We're quite content to rule the wave
   Without a great display;
We're known to be extremely brave;
   But take the sword away.

We give a shrug when pipe and drum
   Play up a favourite air;

We think our barracks are become
 More ugly than they were;
We laugh to see the banners float;
 We loathe the charger's bray;
We don't admire a scarlet coat;
 Do take the sword away!

Let Portugal have rulers twain,
 Let Greece go on with none,
Let Popery sink or swim in Spain
 While we enjoy the fun;
Let Turkey tremble at the knout,
 Let Algiers lose her Dey,
Let Paris turn her Bourbons out;
 Bah! take the sword away.

Our honest friends in Parliament
 Are looking vastly sad;
Our farmers say with one consent
 It's all immensely bad;
There was a time for borrowing,
 And now it's time to pay;
A budget is a serious thing;
 So, take the sword away.

And oh the bitter tears we wept
 In those our days of fame—

The dread that o'er our heart-strings crept
    With every post that came—
The home-affections waged and lost,
    In many a far-off fray—
The price that British glory cost!
    Ah, take the sword away!

We've plenty left to hoist the sail,
    Or dare the dangerous breach,
And Freedom breathes in every gale
    That wanders round our beach.
When Duty bids us dare or die,
    We'll fight, another day;
But till we know the reason why,
    Take—take the sword away!

POLITICAL AND OCCASIONAL POEMS

PART II.

1830—1834.

I.

THE NEW ORDER OF THINGS.

[This poem appeared, 9th December 1830 (four days later than the date of the letter given in the Preface, in which the author announced his intention to accept the offer of a seat for St. Germains), in the *Albion*, a London morning journal of some pretension, though not of large circulation; but far superior in appearance, at this time, to the *Morning Post*. The signature Z was affixed; which I judge to have been a printer's way of representing the initial used by Praed in the *London Magazine*, namely, ℨ.

Lord Tenterden was Chief Justice of the King's Bench. Brougham's peerage, his elevation to the woolsack, and his curious speeches preceding this appointment, were still a nine days' wonder.—The Three per Cents. did not decline much—only from 83 to 82—in consequence of the change of ministry.]

"Incipient magni procedere menses."—*Virg.*

WE'RE sick of this distressing state
   Of order and repose;
We have not had enough of late
   Of blunders, or of blows;
We can't endure to pass our life
   In such a humdrum way;
We want a little pleasant strife—
   The Whigs are in to-day!

Our worthy fathers were content
    With all the world's applause;
They thought they had a parliament,
    And liberty, and laws.
It's no such thing; we've wept and groaned
    Beneath a despot's sway;
We've all been whipped, and starved, and stoned—
    The Whigs are in to-day!

We used to fancy Englishmen
    Had broken Europe's chain,
And won a battle, now and then,
    Against the French in Spain;
Oh no! we never ruled the waves,
    Whatever people say;
We've all been despicable slaves—
    The Whigs are in to-day!

It's time for us to see the things
    Which other folk have seen;
It's time we should cashier our kings,
    And build our guillotine;
We'll abrogate Police and Peers,
    And vote the Church away;
We'll hang the parish overseers —
    The Whigs are in to-day!

We'll put the landlords to the rout;
    We'll burn the College Halls;
We'll turn St. James's inside out,
    And batter down St. Paul's.
We'll hear no more of Bench or Bar;
    The troops shall have no pay:
We'll turn adrift our men of war—
    The Whigs are in to-day!

We fear no bayonet or ball
    From those who fight for hire;
For Baron Brougham has told them all
    On no account to fire.
Lord Tenterden looks vastly black;
    But Baron Brougham, we pray,
Will strip the ermine from his back—
    The Whigs are in to-day!

Go pluck the jewels from the Crown,
    The colours from the mast,
And let the Three per Cents. come down—
    We can but break at last.
If Cobbett is the first of men,
    The second is Lord Grey;
Oh must we not be happy, when
    The Whigs are in to-day!

II.

THE CONVERT.

[*Albion*, 26th Jan. 1831. This piece depicts the excited suspense with which the forthcoming Whig Reform Bill was anticipated. The parallel between "Mr. Grey,"—the Mr. Grey of 1806, and "his son," *i.e.*, Lord Howick, must be read in the light of the inveterate unpopularity of the father's opposition to the French war, and of the somewhat advanced views in which the son, at this time, was considered to indulge.]

Good Lady Grace, the charming Blue,
   Who lately loved, in Grosvenor Square,
To lecture to a favoured few
   On birds and fishes, light and air,
Now flings her learned toys away,
   And spells the wisdom of the *Sun*,
And whispers fifty times a day,
   "Dear cousin, *something* must be done!"

She fears the rabble scarcely grow
   A jot less apt to drink and swear;
She vows that Hume and Brougham and Co.
   Are just as shocking as they were;

What once she said of Mr. Grey
  She says as plainly of his son ;
She talks of Cobbett with dismay :
  But bless her! *something* must be done.

She thinks as fondly as she thought
  Of those that sailed with old Pellew ;
She can't conceive that bondsmen fought
  With Wellington at Waterloo ;
She boasts of Britain's old renown,
  Her dangers dared, her laurels won,
Her blameless Church, her bloodless Crown ;
  Alas! but *something* must be done.

She finds that speeches still are made,
  And laws, and quartern loaves, and rhymes ;
She finds the Three per Cents. are paid,
  As they were paid in olden times ;
She don't believe she's older now
  Than when she laughed at Canning's fun ;
But yet, no matter why or how,
  She's sure that *something* must be done.

Come, ye who have been blind so long,
  And see, by wisdom's modern light,

Whatever has been, may be wrong,
　　Whatever is not, must be right.
Lord Brougham is in Lord Eldon's place;
　　The Whig millennium is begun;
Who would not vote, with Lady Grace,
　　That somehow *something* must be done?

III.
ODE TO POPULARITY.

[*Albion*, 5th May, 1831. The Reform Bill was introduced on the 1st March, and speedily altered the whole aspect of politics. The second reading passed, by one vote, on the 21st; and a month later, the carrying of General Gascoigne's amendment decided Ministers to dissolve Parliament. The election that followed was in full progress when this piece was written: it resulted in the general triumph of the Reformers.—Sir James Graham was now First Lord of the Admiralty; he had attempted a nautical simile, in his speech on the second reading, and had broken down badly. —Sir Thomas Denman was Attorney-General; the allusion in his case is to a passage in his speech on the trial of Queen Caroline.— The riot in which the windows of Apsley House were first broken took place April 27th: the *Times* of the 28th contained no mention of it, but devoted several columns to a Southwark election meeting, at which a Colonel Leslie Grove Jones, author of some letters in its columns, signed "A Radical," was announced as a candidate for the seat previously held by Sir Robert Wilson. Sir Robert, formerly a popular idol, was discarded for voting with General Gascoigne. The Colonel, however, did not stand, Lord Brougham having secured the nomination for his own brother. Next day, the *Times* made a sneering allusion to the Duke's broken windows, and intimated that it was his own fault, for not illuminating. But the newspaper people must have known, what the mob did not, that the Duchess was at the moment lying dead in the house. The October after, the mob, thus encouraged, went back and broke the windows again. Then the Duke put up his well-known iron shutters.—St. John Long was a quack doctor of handsome person, whose treatment consisted in putting a large blister on the bodies of the poor women who were duped by him. Two died, and he was tried for manslaughter, but acquitted; the support of some ladies who still believed in him contributed largely to this result.—Hunt, a leading Radical, and manufacturer of blacking, had defeated Mr. Stanley for Preston the year before; but, once in Parliament, he disappointed his admirers, by attacking the Reform Bill, as a sham.]

> "Quis multâ gracilis te puer in rosâ
> Perfusus liquidis urget odoribus,
> Grato, Pyrrha, sub antro?"—Hor., I. 3.

O FONDEST—and O frailest fair
That ever made a poet swear,
   Bewitching Popularity!
O patroness of songs and scents,
Of budgets and disfranchisements,
   Of treason and vulgarity—

Tell me whom now your fickle pen
Pronounces first of mortal men
   In magazine or journal?
For whom the golden lute you wake,
And whose renown you mean to make
   For just nine weeks eternal?

Dote you on Grey's experienced brow,
Because he's quite as silly now
   As erst our fathers found him?
Or do you lead the approving cheer
When Baron Brougham, the peerless peer,
   Is flinging dirt around him?

ODE TO POPULARITY.

Does soft Sir James, by talking big
Of rope and cable, sloop and brig,
   Persuade you he's a hero?
Or does Sir Thomas please you more
By telling, as he told before,
   The history of Nero?

O Waterloo! You used to say
You never would forget the day
   That cracked the French cuirasses;
But Wednesday last, at half-past ten,
You let the ragged gentlemen
   Smash all his Grace's glasses.

You know you've jilted St. John Long,
And bidden Southwark's noisy throng
   Send poor Sir Robert packing;
You know, without a reason why,
You're burning Hunt in effigy,
   And leaving off his blacking.

Happy on whom untried you smile!
He dreams not for how short a while
   You solemnize the wedding;
How soon you jump from wreaths to stones,
From Wellington to Colonel Jones,
   From kissing to beheading.

Such stormy waves are not for me;
As Graham says, I've seen the sea
　Suck down the struggling packet;
And I renounce the sail and oar,
And hang to dry upon the shore
　My trousers and my jacket.

IV.
THE COMPLAINT OF LIBERTY.

[*Albion*, 4th June, 1831.—The violence which accompanied this general election was something unprecedented in England. For the provocative article which appeared in the *Times*, see Part III., No. I., Note. An elaborate system of "exclusive dealing" was explained and recommended by a Glasgow paper.—Lafayette (*see* Part I., No. IV.) was now a leader of Opposition, under the Monarchy of July ; and was advocating the annexation of Belgium, at the risk of war with England. Latitte, the well-known banker, was Prime Minister when the year opened, and a very weak one. He suffered Casimir Périer and other sensible men, opposed to war, to leave his ministry, and was then himself upset March 13th, by a street riot in Paris, directed rather against the Legitimists than against himself. He afterwards put up for Speaker, and was supported by the Opposition, against the official candidate started by Périer, who succeeded him as Minister ; but he failed of election. The recorder of London in 1818 was Sir John Silvester. —For Joseph Hume and his Greek scrip, see Part I., No. VI.— Jerry is Jeremy Bentham, the assertor of "the greatest happiness of the greatest number," the utilitarian principle in morals.—At the Surrey Sessions, July 4th, the Rev. R. Taylor, a clergyman who had abandoned his religion, was convicted of blasphemy, in exhibiting himself at the Rotunda, in the Borough, dressed up like a Bishop, and thus going through some profane parody of public worship. His defence was, that he was opposed to priests. Hume brought his case before the House of Commons, August 15.—The *Courier* was a paper honoured by Coleridge's political writing in former days, but had become a Ministerial journal of the most conventional type of Toryism, and, more recently, an equally ministerial Whig organ.—The sympathies of William IV. with the popular movement were not altogether imaginary; but the *Times* was just now making capital out of his having dissolved Parliament, by exaggerating them.—Dr. (afterwards Sir John) Bowring was long editor of the *Westminster Review*, and a consistent follower of Bentham, whose works he edited. He was also a persevering writer of verse, original and translated —*invitâ Minervâ*.]

"Lord!" said the little woman, "this can be none of I "—*Old Song*.

"O LIBERTY! whose radiant charms
    Were so adored by Thebes and Sparta—
Bright patroness of arts and arms,
    And authoress of Magna Charta—
Nymph! for whose sake, as we are taught,
    In Plutarch's entertaining stories,
Speeches were made, and battles fought,
    By Greek and Roman, Whigs and Tories;

"Come hither with your pen and sword,
    Your russet garb and mess of pottage;
Leave the wild Arab's wandering horde,
    Or the rude Switzer's humble cottage;
Let Lafayette console Lafitte;
    Let Congress sit a day without you;
Smile, smile, for once, on Downing Street
    I want to write an ode about you!"

She came—she answered. Well I know
    The Speaker's awful call to order;

THE COMPLAINT OF LIBERTY.   135

I heard, some thirteen years ago,
    A sentence from the late Recorder;
I know how hoarse the cheerers are,
    When Whig lords prate of right intention;
But, oh! that fearful voice was far
    More fearful than the sounds I mention.

" I come," she said, " the same who erst
    Held talk with Xenophon and Plato;
Taught Brutus to be firm, and nurst
    The fire of high resolve in Cato;
The same who on your island rock
    Have mocked the hand of sceptred power;
Who went with Sidney to the block,
    And with the Bishops to the Tower.

" Alas! my handmaids, in such days,
    Were Wisdom, Order, and Sobriety;
What loathsome change! My Broughams and Greys
    Have dragged me into strange society;
Treason and Strife invoke my name
    In their dark plots and drunken quarrels;
I'm growing weary of my fame;
    And Jove! how ill I look in laurels!

" I am not what I was; I throw
    Prodigious stones in Clare and Kerry;

I cheat the Greeks with prudent Joe;
   I maximize with sapient Jerry;
Last winter, I confess, I taught
   The labouring class the art of arson,
And oft on Sundays I've been caught
   With Taylor screaming out " No parson ! "

" It's true that still the schoolboy's prayers
   Come up to me in so-so Latin;
And still the lying *Courier* swears
   That all my rags are silk and satin;
And I've a friend at Court, I think;
   But he will doom me to the halter,
When once he hears me in my drink
   Speak out about the throne and altar.

" Farewell ! my anguish would defy
   E'en Althorp's powers of clear expression;
I'm quite convinced that I shall die
   Before the closing of the session;
I'd go with pleasure to the grave;
   But oh ! the thought is overpowering —
They tell me I am sure to have
   An epitaph from Doctor Bowring ! "

V.

WHY AND WHEREFORE.

[From the *Albion* of June 6th, 1831.—" The Schoolmaster abroad " was a phrase of Brougham's, used in connection with the work of the Society for the Diffusion of Useful Knowledge, carried on at this time by a committee of which he was chairman, in the buildings of the London University.—Lord Palmerston, the Foreign Secretary, and Mr. Charles Grant (afterwards Lord Glenelg) the President of the Board of Control, had been members of Tory administrations before they passed, on Canning's death, into the Whig ranks. Robert Grant, brother to Charles, better known as a hymn-writer, was Judge Advocate General, and Lord Goderich (See Part I., No. VII.) Secretary for the Colonies.—Sir G. Cockburn had been roughly handled in an election riot at Plymouth, and Sir Roger Gresley of Drakelow, at Derby.]

"Come, your reason, Jack, your reason."—*Shakespeare.*

I was a Tory once, you know,
A king and constitution man ;
But that was many years ago,
Before the march of mind began.
'Twas very well to be a dunce
When no one asked me why or how ;
I own, I was a Tory once ;
But Lord ! I'm not a Tory now.

The schoolmaster's abroad, you see;
   And, when the people hear him speak,
They all insist on being free,
   And reading Homer in the Greek;
The Bolton weavers seize the pen,
   The Sussex farmers scorn the plough;
One must advance with other men;
   And so, I'm not a Tory now.

Look at the papers! There you'll find
   The *Courier* full of Cobbett's taunts;
Lord Palmerston has changed his mind;
   And what's become of both the Grants?
How should I hope to stem the storm
   Which makes such mighty statesmen bow?
Why, Goderich is for this Reform!
   And who would be a Tory now?

And then, the people are stark mad!
   They go about with sticks and stones!
And these accounts are very bad
   Of broken glass and broken bones;
Poor Cockburn had some shocking hurts;
   I never could endure a row;
They tore Sir Roger Gresley's skirts!
   No, no, I'm not a Tory now.

You know my nephew—clever youth—
   He came last year from Harrow school;

He's done a pamphlet which, in truth,
   Makes out that I've been quite a fool.
Pray read this little page, about
   The healthy trunk and rotten bough;
It proves, beyond the smallest doubt,
   No patriot is a Tory now.

I'll introduce you to my wife;
   She brought me fifty thousand pounds;
And she's the blessing of my life,
   Although she made me cut the hounds.
She reads the *Herald* every day,
   And talks—'twould do you good, I vow;
She's very partial to Lord Grey;
   How can I be a Tory now?

Tom wants a living—what of that?
   Brougham never heard me urge his claims.
And Hal's appointed to the Rat!
   But—Sir! I never asked Sir James.
Oh no! I like the Church and Laws;
   And—candidly, you must allow
That I have shown sufficient cause
   Why I am not a Tory now.

VI.

KING ALFRED'S BOOK.

[While the second Reform Bill was passing through Committee, a new weekly paper was started under the name, by no means new, of the *Alfred*, upon strict Conservative principles. This poem was written for the second number, and appeared in it, 7th August 1831. The portraits sketched are, it will be perceived, those of Wellington, Peel, Grey, Russell, Durham and Brougham.—The "ruler" was the scale adopted by the Government in calculating what boroughs should, and what should not be disfranchised. It was a combination of the population and rating tests, and the calculations, not being very easily intelligible, were much assailed.]

"His mighty genius prompted him to undertake a most great and necessary work, which he is said to have executed in as masterly a manner;—no less than to new model the Constitution,—to rebuild it on a plan that should endure for ages."—*History of England*.

I saw in a dream, on a summer day,
The tomb where the Saxon Solon lay;
And thither the prince of the land was led,
With the robe on his shoulder, the crown on his head;
And they bade him draw from its secret nook
The volume of law, King Alfred's Book.

KING ALFRED'S BOOK.

He held the tome in his feeble grasp ;
He broke the seals, and he snapped the clasp.
Long years had marred on the dim, dim page
The treasured truth of the Chief and Sage;
And whose were the hands that undertook
To write new words in the holy book ?

A laurelled warrior thither came ;
How the deep heart thrilled as they named his name !
He gazed on the volume of right and law,
And he turned away from the sight he saw,
Falsehood and blame he would rather brook,
Than sully one page of the time-worn book.

A statesman came, and through the crowd
The murmur of hope was heard aloud ;
" Let him trace but a line, and the peril is o'er,
And the leaves shall sleep where they slept before."
Power and praise his heart forsook ;
He turned away from the fearful book.

I saw a hoary dotard stand,
And grasp the pen in his feeble hand ;
He had written a rare bold text, they said,
Ere the white snows fell on his plotting head ;

But now he was grey, and his fingers shook,
As he scrawled and scrawled on the sacred book.

"I have brought," quoth a schoolboy, "this ruler of
　　mine,
To rule for the letters a fair straight line."
He babbled of parish, he babbled of town,
And the ruler went up, and the ruler went down;
So crooked was never the crookedest crook
As the line he drew on the wondrous book.

There came a sallow penman now,
With a sneer on his lip and a scowl on his brow;
So quick was his hand, that you saw at a glance
He had learned of the cunning scribes of France:
" Might " for " right " his haste mistook,
And " treason " for " reason " he wrote in the book.

And there was a schoolmaster, tall and thin,
With a solemn smile on his nose and chin;
He smoothed the leaf, and he mended the pen,
And he rapped the knuckles now and then;
" How scared," quoth he," the dolts will look
If ever they read what they write in the book !"

" Oh, write what ye may, or write what ye will,"
Said the cry of a mob from a cotton-mill;

"The words may be grave, and the wit may be
   good;
But we're building the gallows, and lighting the
   wood:
The bird to the snare, and the fish to the hook,
And a rope for the clerks, and a fire for the book!"

VII.

INTENTIONS.

A REMONSTRANCE IN THE VENTILATOR.

[Written for the *Alfred*, August 21st, 1831. The "Ventilator" was the ladies' gallery of the old House of Commons, and it was from the accidental circumstance that its occupants were invisible to those on the floor, that the curious superstition arose, which required a grating to be prefixed to the accommodation provided for ladies in the new House of Commons.

The necessities of debate required that Lord Althorp should be Leader of the House of Commons, with the office of Chancellor of the Exchequer; but his powers as a financier were limited, and Mr. Poulett Thomson, an M.P. of experience in the City, was made Vice-President of the Board of Trade, with the view of supplying the deficiency. The arrangement was not successful. The first budget of the Whig administration, an ambitious attempt at the readjustment of three millions of taxation, failed through the opposition of commercial men to the proposed tax on transfers; and a further modification, in regard to the timber duties, was defeated on a division. In the result, the scheme was practically abandoned.—In Lord Grey's administration were included a son, son-in-law, and two brothers-in-law of his own, besides several cousins of his wife's; and the names of Grey, Ponsonby, Lambton and Ellice occur rather oftener than could be accounted for by the Theory of Chances, in the "promotions and preferments" column of 1830-1834. Hunt attacked him for this, during the Preston Election, and he replied in the Lords, 13th December, 1830.—The revolt of Belgium from Holland, favoured by the

French, for whom Talleyrand was ambassador in England, was now in progress. The Whig ministry sided with the Belgians, and upset the Vienna settlement, so far as Holland was concerned.—The Marquis of Lansdowne was President of the Council].

Now don't abuse us, Fanny, don't;
   You're really too provoking!
I won't sit by, I vow I won't,
   To hear your idle croaking.
You seem to think the world is mad
   For places and for pensions,
And won't believe—it's quite too bad—
   That Whigs have good intentions.

I know that Denman *is* too rash,
   And Graham not *too* witty;
I know we hear prodigious trash
   From members for the City;
Young Thomson is a financier
   Of rather small dimensions;
Lord Althorp is not vastly clear:
   But all have bright intentions.

The Budget *was* a slight mistake;
   You call it quite correctly;
But then confess, for candour's sake,
   We gave it up directly.

They laughed it down on every side,
　　Forgetting their dissensions;
But not a single man denied
　　It shewed the best intentions.

The Premier *has* been kind, I own,
　　To most of his connections;
But Hunt, you see, was quite alone
　　In making harsh reflections.
The blockhead ought to go to school
　　And study his declensions;
Then he would judge by better rule
　　A statesman's grand intentions.

It's true we've not been doing *much*
　　To make the Frenchman humble;
And after all those dear, dull Dutch
　　Have cause enough to grumble.
We cannot see—who says we can?
　　Through Talleyrand's inventions;
For he's a wicked, clever man;
　　And we—have pure intentions.

And Fanny—as for this Reform,
　　Which Peel pronounces treason,
Indeed I think you make a storm
　　Without sufficient reason.

The Bill is full of faults no doubt,
    But, as my husband mentions,
One would not have a fault struck out
    Which flows from just intentions.

Some say the Bill destroys the Crown;
    Some swear it galls the people;
Some see the peerage tumbling down,
    Some fear for Church and steeple.
There may be good substantial cause
    For many apprehensions;
But *coûte que coûte*, in every clause
    There's proof of right intentions.

We can't expect that Brougham and Hume
    Will lay their horrid plans down.
But, dearest love, you won't assume
    The fault is with Lord Lansdowne!
They can't do harm—or if they do,
    In spite of wise preventions,
I hate their schemes, but, *entre nous*,
    I honour their intentions.

VIII.

THE BEGGAR'S PETITION.

[From the *Albion*, 22nd Aug., 1831.—Early in this month an address, asking for an audience, was signed by twelve Irish members, and presented to the Prime Minister. The interview took place on the 12th, at Lord Grey's private residence; when about twenty members attended, and Lord Killeen, as their spokesman demanded a gradual reduction of the yeomanry, with a view to its dissolution. Lord Grey in his answer refused, with "lofty civility," to grant their request, while promising a measure for "regulation" of the force. Upon this a communication appeared in the *Times*, signed by twenty-one M.P's, O'Connell being one; it said: "Ireland will not be contented with a flippant heedlessness of her grievances on the part of Mr. Stanley in the House of Commons; the harsh frivolity of his demeanour has caused a great deal of perhaps disproportioned resentment; but Irishmen are not skilled in the just mensuration between an affront and its retribution." The paper went on to threaten the Government with opposition, unless the new regulations were immediately introduced. On the 15th, on the committee stage of an unimportant "Lords Lieutenant of Ireland (Counties) Bill," O'Connell suddenly attacked the Government with much vehemence. It was natural that this split should be regarded by opponents as indicating an impatience on his part for place; but it was, no doubt, more justly to be attributed to his having become convinced that Lord Grey was neither to be intimidated nor cajoled. From this time his efforts were directed towards a decapitation of the ministry.— O'Connell was at this time accustomed to sit upon the Opposition

THE BEGGAR'S PETITION.   149

Benches. Mr. Knight, M.P. for Wallingford, Sir Edward Sugden, afterwards Lord St. Leonards, Mr. Croker, ex-Secretary of the Admiralty, and Sir Charles Wetherell, the "last of the Boroughbridges," as he called himself, were all Tories sitting at this period below the gangway, and belonging rather to the school of Eldon and Wellington, than of Peel.—Lord Duncannon, eldest son of Lord Bessborough, and a connection of Lady Grey's, was the Treasury Whip.—Mr. H. Grattan, afterwards an M.P., unlike his father, was notable only for the quantity of his speeches.—Derrynane Abbey, near Killarney, was the seat of the O'Connells, as long as rent—of any kind—was regularly paid in Kerry.]

"Extremum Tanain si biberes, Lyce," etc.—HOR., III. 10.

IF you were placed in some rude station
    Where no man sighs for stars or garters,
Where Papists shrink from agitation,
    And Whigs have some respect for charters,
Still, still, Lord Grey, I'd not be guessing
    Why, in your foolish prides and glories,
You'd keep a friend without a blessing,
    Placeless and payless, with the Tories.

Ah, don't you see with what barbarity
    The members all around me treat me?
Knight's look is not a look of charity;
    Sir Edward Sugden longs to beat me;
Croker, bad luck to him, is witty,
    And Wetherell is entirely teazing,
And Peel, without a spark of pity,
    Sets, now and then, my heart's blood freezing.

Och ! don't be proud !   Sure, cool reflection
    Should cure your scoffing and your scorning;
The wheel may turn, and my affection,
    Just like the Bill, get lost, some morning:
And though the Duke might look severely
    On me and my Associators,
Musha ! your father's son should dearly
    Esteem all demagogues and traitors.

Be warned ; though you are cold and cruel,
    Though deputations don't persuade you,
Though you are yet unshaken, jewel,
    By all the compliments I've paid you ;
Though you are deaf to Grattan's speeches
    Which flow as ceaseless as the Shannon,
And blind to those unwilling breaches
    Of discipline in sad Duncannon,

Be wise in time. O stubborn-hearted !
    Regardless, as an oak, of blarney !
Deaf, as the adders, that departed
    Some years ago, from sweet Killarney !
Be wise in time ! You won't ? Oh murther !
    An't we all patriots, stout and manly ?
My Lord, we won't put up much further
    With bows, and frowns, and Master Stanley.

IX.

SPEECH OF THE IRISH SECRETARY IN DEFENCE OF THE LORD LIEUTENANT.

[*Albion*, Aug. 24th, 1831.—Irish affairs continued troublesome to the Ministry. On the 23rd Mr. Stanley had to defend the Government of Ireland against a charge of interference in the recent election for Dublin. Mr. Long, a well-known coachmaker, had been canvassed by Captain Hart "on the part of the Lord Lieutenant," the Marquis of Anglesey, for the Reform candidates. The Viceroy "had expressed to the Captain his *wishes* for their success." In consequence of reports that *threats* had been used, Sir John Byng went to Lord Anglesey, and obtained a paper stating, under the form of "his Lordship's feelings," that he certainly *expected* his tradesmen to vote in a particular way. This was communicated to Mr. Long, *by way of reassuring him;* and Mr. Stanley loudly complained that Mr. Long, in revealing the nature of this communication, "had turned upon" Lord Anglesey.— Baron Tuyll, a Hanoverian, private secretary to the Viceroy, also canvassed; and had interviews at the castle with two of the police magistrates, Messrs. Tyndale and Studdart, in which, as Mr. Stanley admitted, "his observations were not discreet;" but what they were he did not say.—Basseggio was a fashionable hairdresser, who held a small place in the Castle household as a member of the "Battle-axe Guard"; from this he was dismissed for voting Tory: but on its being discovered that he had paid for his place, he was promptly reinstated. In replying, Mr. Stanley "thought he might pass over the case of Basseggio."—The question was treated as a motion for Lord Anglesey's dismissal, and rejected by 207 to 66.—Cold Blow Lane leads from Donnybrook to Milltown, and may be taken as a local synonym for the former classical locality.—Subsequently a Committee found that undue influence had been used, the members were unseated, and two anti-reformers returned.]

    "On, Stanley, on."—*Marmion*

Sir, we have closed our long campaign
Against the troops of Cold Blow Lane;
We've done with Mr. Grattan's votes,
Their venal hearts and ragged coats;
And it is time for me to show
The Castle folk are unsunned snow,
And prove, howe'er the case appears,
His Lordship never interferes.

One Long, a mean and paltry knave,
By reason of the vote he gave,
Has lost most justly, as he feels,
The mending of his Lordship's wheels.
Out on the villain! By my troth,
We won't believe a tradesmen's oath,
When he, the Prince of British Peers,
Declares he never interferes!

As for the lines his Lordship wrote,
To say that every honest vote
Was, as was very right and fair,
Requested here, expected there—

I own it was extremely wrong
To be so kind to Mr. Long ;
Yet in that letter, who that hears
Will say, his Lordship interferes?

And then, the melancholy fates
Or those poor perjured magistrates,
Who were so wonderfully rude,
And talked of friends, and gratitude :
The men, it's certain, went and did
Exactly as the men were bid ;
But Sir, with Mr. Tyndale's tears
The Castle never interferes.

Honest Basseggio next attacks—
The barber—with his battle-axe !
Who vomits speeches brave and big
Against whate'er is wise and Whig ;
I'm sure that none who know the case,
And how the barber lost his place,
Can deem with such plebeian fears
His Lordship ever interferes.

Oh, I appeal to all the fame
That crowns that noble person's name ;
And I appeal to Captain Hart,
Who could not play the bully's part ;

And I appeal to Baron Tuyll,
Who sealed his lips up all the while;
And I appeal to those loud cheers—
His Lordship never interferes.

All people, Mr. Speaker, know
Which way his Lordship's wishes go;
And Government, it's also known,
Do as they will with what's their own:
And since my noble friend is right
To interfere with all his might—
I care not for those vulgar sneers—
He never, never interferes.

X.

SPEECH DELIVERED BY A WORTHY ALDERMAN, SEVERAL TIMES, IN COMMITTEE ON THE REFORM BILL.

[Written for the *Alfred*, 28th August, 1831.—Four Aldermen, Wood, Waithman, Thompson, and Venables, sat for the City; but Waithman was the hero of this parody. See his speeches of July 19th and 22nd, and of August 3rd. On one occasion Lord John Russell had to appeal to the House against the obstruction caused by a long conversation between Waithman and Wetherell.—Mr. Bernal was the Chairman of Committees.]

I DO not rise—I never will—
To make a speech about the Bill;
I only want to urge once more
What I have often urged before;
It can't be doubted or denied,
That members on the other side
Are talking, talking, day by day,
Just for the purpose of delay.

Why, Sir, the nation, as we know,
Passed all the Bill some months ago;

And my constituents, Sir, object
To any members who reflect;
And therefore I am bold to state
I disapprove of all debate,
And sit in absolute dismay
When I observe so much delay.

Oh Mr. Bernal, don't forget
The burden of our monstrous debt!
Consider, Sir, how every year
Taxation's growing more severe;
I must assert that I, for one,
Believe the country quite undone;
Some fools dispute it—so they may;
But I protest against delay.

Why, Sir, I'll venture to advance
We were some years at war with France;
And now Britannia's flag is furled,
And we're at peace with all the world.
All honourable members ought
To think as much as I have thought;
Then they would work the shortest way,
And pass the Bill without delay.

And I'm prepared to prove, I trust,
That every word is true and just

SPEECH BY A WORTHY ALDERMAN. 157

In all the speeches I have made
On import and on export trade.
Official values, I admit,
Are things beyond my humble wit;
But all these things, I'm sure, display
The dangerous folly of delay.

And Sir, I don't dislike a clause
Because it's full of faults and flaws;
And Sir, I think it's most perverse
To prate of better, or of worse;
And Sir, I find, though members laugh,
Too many lawyers here, by half;
And Sir, I shall advise Lord Grey
To gag them all without delay.

I should be very glad to touch
Upon the French, the Poles, and Dutch
And tell you why I think it sin
To let the foreign silks come in;
But I have always thought it right
To keep the question full in sight
And I should be ashamed to play
The game of men who want delay

Sir, I conclude, as I began,
By begging every honest man

To end the nation's doubts and fears,
And hold his tongue, and stop his ears.
Of argument we've had enough ;
It's very sudorific stuff ;
And I have one thing more to say—
I can't account for this delay.

XI.

THE BILL, THE WHOLE BILL, AND NOTHING BUT THE BILL.

[*Albion*, 26th September, 1831.—This skit was written for the Dorsetshire Election, occasioned by the suicide of Mr. Calcraft, in which Lord Ashley was returned, as a Conservative. It had, apparently, a considerable success. Sydney Smith had it in his mind, in making his last Taunton speech, May 1832: "There will be mistakes at first, as there are in all changes: all young ladies will imagine, as soon as this Bill is carried, that they will be instantly married; schoolboys believe that Gerunds and Supines will be abolished, and that currant tarts must ultimately come down in price; the Corporal and the Sergeant are sure of double pay; bad poets are sure of a demand for their epics; fools will be disappointed, as they always are; reasonable men, who know what to expect, will find that a very serious good has been obtained."]

Come listen, come listen, I'm going to sing
A song that's much newer than "God save the King;"
All about what I think of this wonderful Bill,
Which hasn't passed yet—can you guess when it will?
      Derry down.

I hear it's to work us more wonders, some day,
Than Harlequin's wand ever did in the play;

It's to make kings and queens out of Jack and of
    Jill :
Will it ever do this ?   Why, I don't think it will.
                    Derry down.

It's to make us new clothes, as I've heard people tell :
A shirt for myself, and a bonnet for Nell ;
A bonnet with ribbands, a shirt with a frill ;
Will it come to be true ?   I'll be hanged if it will !
                    Derry down.

It's to light us a fire, and lay us a bed ;
It's to pave Holborn Hill with the best wheaten
    bread ;
It's to bring down fine Hollands to nothing a gill—
Believe, if you like ; I'll be whipped if I will.
                    Derry down.

It's to heal all disorders, wherever it goes,
In the feet and the hands, in the eyes and the nose ;
It's to cure gout and ague, instead of a pill.
Some folks say it won't ; but Lord John says it will.
                    Derry down.

It's to give to the troops, and the tars of the fleet,
No jacket to wear, and no pudding to eat ;

When we've just done away with the mess and the
  drill,
Will we lick the Mounseers? Ask the Duke if we
  will.
Derry down.

It's to get us a parson, as good as St. Paul,
Who won't want a lodging or dinner at all;
He'll teach us our duties and preach us our fill,
But as for his tithes—he may starve, if he will.
Derry down.

It's to give us—good luck to it! freedom and trade;
Our goods will be sold, and our debts will be paid.
It will conjure up wealth for the ledger and till—
I wish I could only find out how it will!
Derry down.

It will bring health to sickness, and warmth to the
  cold,
And wit to the foolish, and youth to the old,
And soup to the saucepan, and grist to the mill—
Fine words, honest friends! But I doubt if it will.
Derry down.

It's to change, in a minute, one guinea to ten;
It's to marry our daughters to handsome young men;

It's to make me a singer of science and skill.
If you trust all the rest, don't you trust that it will?
       Derry down.

And now here's success to the ancient old cause
Of the King and the People, the Land and the Laws;
And the Devil fly away with the Whigs and the Bill!
(Don't say that I said it) I fancy he will!
       Derry down.

XII.
REASONS FOR NOT RATTING.

[The Reform Bill had now gone up to the Lords. Lord Dudley and Ward was a Canningite who had not become a Whig. This is from the *Albion* of 7th October.—The passage quoted is omitted in Hansard, but will be found in the *Times* report.—"Pellew," that is to say, Lord Exmouth, was next neighbour to Mr. Serjeant Praed, the poet's father, at Teignmouth.]

"Sound opinions are like sound wine, they are the better for keeping."—*Speech of Lord Dudley, 5th October,* 1831.

It was my father's wine. Alas,
   It was his chiefest bliss
To fill an old friend's evening glass
   With nectar such as this!
I think I have as warm a heart—
   As kind a friend as he.
Another bumper ere we part!
   Old wine—old wine for me!

In this we toasted William Pitt,
   Whom twenty now outshine;
O'er this we laughed at Canning's wit,
   Ere Hume's was thought as fine.
In this "The King!" "The Church!" "The Laws!"
   Have had their three times three.

Sound wine befits as sound a cause;
    Old wine—old wine for me!

In this, when France in those long wars
    Was beaten black and blue,
We used to drink our troops and tars—
    Our Wellesley and Pellew.
Now, things are changed. Though Britain's fame
    May out of fashion be,
At least my wine remains the same.
    Old wine—old wine for me.

My neighbours, Robinson and Lamb,
    Drink French of last year's growth:
I'm sure, however they may sham,
    It disagrees with both.
I don't pretend to interfere;
    An Englishman is free;
But none of that cheap poison here!
    Old wine—old wine for me.

Some dozens lose, I must allow,
    Something of strength and hue;
And there are vacant spaces now,
    To be filled up with new;
And there are cobwebs round the bins,
    Which some don't like to see;
If these are all my cellar's sins,
    Old wine—old wine for me!

XIII.

THE OLD TORY.

[*Albion*, 29th Nov., 1831.—On 6th Feb., 1832, Praed wrote—" Did I tell you an odd thing that occurred with respect to my squib *The Old Tory?* Sir Robert (Peel) saw it by chance in a provincial paper, cut it out, and brought it to London; and when some of his friends were talking of some articles written or to be written for the London papers, Sir Robert produced this, and said they had nobody in London who could do anything so pointed. Whereupon, after much laughing, he was told that the bairn was rocked in the *Morning Post*, and that the Papa was one of his Glorious Minority!" The *Morning Post*, like the provincial paper, had copied the poem from the *Albion*.—Master Cam is Mr. Hobbouse, the friend of Lord Byron, then M.P. for Westminster.—Mr. Attwood was Chairman of the Birmingham Political Union, which threatened to march on London, 200,000 strong, if the Reform Bill did not pass. " Where are they going to get shoes?" said the Duke of Wellington. Lord J. Russell wrote to them—" It is impossible that the whisper of faction should prevail against the voice of the nation."—Mr. Place, a master tailor, succeeded Sir Francis Burdett, when he resigned the chairmanship of the National Political Union; which he did in disgust at a stipulation that some working men should be included in the Committee. Dr. Carpue kept a private anatomy school; he also headed a Reform Deputation from Westminster, which waited upon Lord Grey.—Lord Morpeth, afterwards Earl of Carlisle, had been an Etonian of rather older standing to Praed. His verses in the " Poetry of the College Magazine," were thought to give promise of distinction.]

"Quo semel est imbuta recens, servabit odorem Testa diu."—Hor.

Aye, chatter, chatter, brother Sam;
    Call Thomson deep and Sheil divine;
And tell us all that Master Cam
    Is quite a Tully in his line.
I'm near threescore; you ought to know
    You can't transplant so old a tree;
I was a Tory long ago;
    You'll hardly make a Whig of me.

Lord Palmerston may turn about,
    And curse the creed he held so long;
And moral Grant may now find out
    That Canning was extremely wrong:
Lansdowne with Waithman may unite,
    And Ministers with mobs agree;
Truth may be falsehood, black grow white,
    But, sir, you make no Whig of me.

You know I never learned to trust
    The wisdom of the Scotch Review;
I worshipped not Napoleon's bust;
    I could not blush for Waterloo:
I'm proud of England's glory still,
    Of laurels won on land and sea;
Call me a bigot if you will,
    But pray don't make a Whig of me.

THE OLD TORY.

I cannot march with Attwood's ranks,
    I cannot write with Russell's pen,
I have no longing for the thanks
    Of very loyal tithing-men;
I cannot wear a civil face
    When Carpue just drops in to tea;
I cannot flatter Mr. Place;
    You'll never make a Whig of me.

I can't admire the Bristol rows,
    Nor call the Common Council wise;
I cannot bow as Burdett bows,
    Nor lie as great O'Connell lies;
And if I wanted place or pay,
    A Baron's robe, or Bishop's see,
I'm not first cousin to Lord Grey—
    Why should you make a Whig of me?

Good brother, 'twere an easier thing
    To make a wit of Joseph Hume,
To make a conjuror of Lord King,
    To make a lawyer of Lord Brougham.
No, Howick will be half his sire,
    And Althorp learn the Rule of Three,
And Morpeth set the Thames on fire,
    Before you make a Whig of me!

XIV.

THE YOUNG WHIG.

[This piece was found among the poet's MSS. It is an altered version of a little trifle printed in the Collected Poems, vol. I., p. 362, called "Anticipations;" and must have been composed in that form, when he entered Parliament, and re-written, in this, soon after. Schedule A of the Reform Bill contained the names of fifty-six boroughs which were entirely disfranchised.]

Oh yes, he is in Parliament,
    He's been returning thanks;
You can't conceive the time he's spent
    In giving people franks;
He's grown a most important man,
    His name's in the *Gazette;*
And, though he swears he never can—
    I'm sure he will—forget.

He talks quite grand of Grant and Grey;
    He jests at Holland House;
He dines extremely every day
    On ortolans and grouse:

Our salads now he will not touch,
    He keeps a different set;
They'll never love him half so much
    As those he must forget!

He used to write the sweetest things,
    In all our Albums, once;
But now his harp has lost the strings;
    His muse is quite a dunce.
We read his speeches in the *Times*,
    And vast renown they get;
But all those dear, delicious rhymes
    All hearts, but mine, forget.

He flirts this year immensely ill;
    His flattery don't improve;
When Weippert plays a gay quadrille,
    He sighs, "I rise to move;"
And when I sing "The Soldier's Tear,"
    The song he called his "pet,"
He comes and whispers "Hear, Lear, hear!
    How can he so forget?

I'm studying now, to please his taste,
    MacCulloch, Bentham, Mill;
To win his smile, I'm making haste
    To understand the Bill;

I read the stuff Reviewers write
    Of corn, and funds, and debt;
Alas, that all I read at night
    With morning I forget!

I wish he'd leave his friend, Lord Brougham,
    The realm's disease to cure;
Wherever else, in him there's room
    For some reform, I'm sure!
His borough is in Schedule A,
    And that's some comfort yet;
'Twill hardly give him time, they say—
    Poor fellow! to forget!

XV.

ODE ADDRESSED TO THE RT. HON. POULETT THOMSON, ON HIS DISCOVERY OF THE FRUCTIFYING PRINCIPLE.

[The division of financial responsibility in the Whig Ministry between Lord Althorp and Mr. Poulett Thomson continued to be unsuccessful. Their second Budget anticipated a surplus for the year 1832-3 of half a million. A question by Mr. Goulburn disclosed the fact that, among others, a mistake of £350,000 had been made, in calculating the estimated amount of the beer duties; and a sharp debate followed. The Vice-President of the Board of Trade came to the assistance of the Chancellor of the Exchequer. " If there was a deficiency, where, he would ask, was that deficiency? Did it consist of money taken from the pockets of the people, and lavished upon undue expenditure or unworthy enterprise, or did it not remain in the pockets of the people, to be drawn thence if the necessities of the State should require it? . . . He was happy to say that it remained in the pockets of the people, there to fructify by use, and to stimulate the efforts of their industry." Peel's reply was crushing: "The Vice-President of the Board of Trade had broached a most extraordinary doctrine he had congratulated the country on the deficiency of £698,000 because it was in fact, 'not lost;' it 'remained in the pockets of the people,' to be extracted on any future occasion. This the Right Honourable gentleman called by a name which he hoped would not soon be forgotten—he called it the *Fructifying Principle!* If he could only establish that principle generally, he would stand a chance of being the most popular man in the three kingdoms; every debtor would only have to tell his too pressing creditor, Do not give yourself any trouble about your principal or interest; for you to say that you are losing money is mere delusion; it is in my pocket, on the Fructifying Principle, ready to be extracted on any future occasion!" This piece appeared next day, 7th February, 1832, in the *Albion*.—Dr. Kitchiner's cookery books assumed for their compiler somewhat more in the way of originality than was fairly due. On the other hand he attributes to Mrs. Glass the time-honoured joke, "First catch your hare," which that lady did not perpetrate.—Mr. Wellesley Pole (see Pt. I., No. XIX.), afterwards Lord Maryborough, and eventually Earl of Mornington, married Miss Tilney Long, a Wiltshire heiress, and spent her fortune. He was satirized in the "Rejected Addresses," during the butterfly stage of his existence—

"Bless every man possessed of aught to give!
Long may Long Tilney Wellesley Long Pole live!"

Daniel Whittle Harvey, afterwards City Commissioner of Police, was M.P. for Colchester; Schonswar for Kingston-upon-Hull; both were, or were supposed to be, in impecunious circumstances. For Alderman Waithman, the city draper, see No. X., and Coleridge's "Essays on His Own Times," p. 769.]

Poulett, our ancestors were fools;
But we have lectures, pamphlets, schools,
    Lord Brougham and Gower Street College;
All patriots learn to read and write;
And bigots shudder at the light
    Of newspapers and knowledge.

Immortal men our Earth have blest;
Great Kitchiner invented yest,
    And made mysterious gravy;

In jet is blazoned Warren's name ;
The safety lamp lights up the fame
  Of good Sir Humphrey Davy.

But round thy temples, Thomson, played
(Young Solon of the Board of Trade)
  A blaze of brighter glory ;
When thou didst make, with wondrous wit,
A surplus of a deficit,
  To bother Whig and Tory.

" Let not the creditor be grieved,
Although his cash be not received ; "
  Oh bliss to hear thee say it !
" How can his interest be worse ?
'Tis fructifying in the purse
  Of those who ought to pay it ! "

The gallery shook at that dark word ;
The chief clerk trembled as he heard ;
  Up started Mr. Speaker :
And thou didst smile on poor Lord A.,
A mild, meek smile, that seemed to say
  " Eureka ! Lo, Eureka ! "

" Henceforth," Long Wellesley Long Pole said,
" Henceforth I shall not hear with dread
  The echoes of my knocker ! "

Quoth Joseph Hume, "I'll bet a pound
The clever boy has somewhere found
   My own new notes on Cocker!"

Harvey and Schonswar cried, "Hear, hear,"
Only poor Waithman did not cheer;
   Ah, whence was Waithman's sorrow?
"I wish," he sighed, "that eight or nine
Good liberal customers of mine
   Mayn't see the *Times* to-morrow!"

Hail, happy Thomson! Fraud and debt
Shall mock the Fleet and the *Gazette*,
   By grace of thine orations;
Fierce Captain Rock, in Clare and Louth,
Shall leave off oaths, and learn to mouth
   Thy limpid lucubrations.

Prate on, prate on, oh! not in vain;
So long as London shall contain
   A seller and a buyer—
Perish Ricardo, perish Mill!
Thy praise shall be recorded still,
   Poulett—the Fructifier!

XVI.

THE DREAM OF A REPORTER.

[*Albion*, 20th February, 1832.—On the 18th the Whig ministry dined at the Mansion House. Sir W. Horne was Solicitor-General.—In 1822 Lord John Russell published "Don Carlos, a Tragedy," which did not contribute to his reputation.—Mr. Calley was M.P. for Cricklade; he was guilty of having, in Committee on the Estimates, suddenly blurted out that—" Honourable members should first pass the Reform Bill, and then he would listen to their speeches with pleasure!"—Hunt was the first M.P. to begin the systematic degradation of the House of Commons by obstructive babbling upon all subjects which he did not (and there were few which he did) understand.—Sir H. Parnell wrote "A Plan of Financial Reform," upon which Lord Althorp's first Budget was based. He was also the mover of the resolution which brought the Whigs into power, and had been rewarded with the Office of Secretary at War.—Sheil, an eloquent Irish M.P., was O'Connell's most conspicuous lieutenant.—Lord Grey resided at East Sheen during the London Session. He had warned the Bishops, in introducing the Reform Bill, to "set their house in order."—The Queen was known to favour the Anti-Reforming party, and was repeatedly attacked in the *Times*.—Several new peers had lately been made, to grace the Coronation.]

"Dreams being, as plays are, the representation of things which do not really happen."—*Johnson's Dictionary*.

THE speech was dull, the speech was long;
Deep languor o'er my senses crept;

I know it was extremely wrong,
   But there I nodded, yawned and slept.
I slept. By Lethe's drowsy lake!
   I hold him not of woman born,
Who can contrive to keep awake
   Through more than half an hour of Horne.

I dreamed a dream. There came a change
   On day and night, on heaven and earth;
Whate'er I saw was new and strange;
   All Nature had a second birth;
Antiquity began to stare,
   Arithmetic was all aghast,
For round was turning into square,
   And two and two were five, at last!

Above, below, methought I saw
   More marvels than the Muse can name;
A Denman with a little law;
   A Harvey with some sense of shame.
Methought I heard Lord Althorp say
   A thing which Canning might have said,
And found that Lord John Russell's play
   Was pretty generally read.

Calley was sober; Hunt was dumb;
   Sir Henry Parnell had no plan;

Sheil reasoned; Stanley was become
  A most good-natured gentleman;
There were no robbers left in Greece;
  There were no papists left in Rome;
And Clare and Kerry were at peace;
  So, also, was thy nose, Lord Brougham!

I too was changed. I wrote a speech
  To prove my grandfather a slave;
I taught what Scotch Reviewers teach;
  I raved as Bowring's pupils rave.
At city feasts I learnt to bless
  The memory of immortal Cade,
And "fructified" with great success,
  One morning, at the Board of Trade.

I felt that Whiggism was divine;
  I bowed immensely low at Sheen;
I praised Lord Holland's wit and wine;
  I wrote a libel on the Queen.
I whispered that the Bishops want
  The schoolmaster's instructive rod,
And vowed that it is monstrous cant
  To talk of Providence or God.

Apt student in the Liberal school,
  I earned my patron's worthless pay;

I took a cheque from Wellesley Pole,
    And worse, a title from Lord Grey.
Alas, it was a dream of fear,
    A dream of guilt, a dream of pain;
For all O'Connell bagged last year
    I would not dream that dream again!

XVII.
THE NEW LIGHT.

BY AN ADMIRER OF JOSEPH HUME, ESQ., M.P.

[In a debate on the Russo-Dutch loan, July 17, 1832, Mr. Hume said—"He was anxious to state the reasons which induced him to vote on the present question, first against Ministers, then with them; and also his reasons for the vote he was going to give that evening. . . . He had come down to the House last Thursday as determined as man could be to vote against the proposal of the noble Lord, the Chancellor of the Exchequer; but, when he found how he was surrounded, and saw that the case was altogether against Ministers, he was unwilling to become a party to that proceeding, which could not fail to bring about their resignation. Honourable members may laugh, but I repeat, that I voted against the Tories, whom I on the present question verily believe to be right, and with the Ministers, whom I as verily believe to be wrong, solely because I did not wish to turn out the present Ministry. For this, I know, I am accused of surrendering my judgment. What do I care about my judgment? Why, sir, I have surrendered my judgment dozens of times for these selfsame Ministers! Over and over again I have pledged myself that black was white, and white was black, merely to get them out of a scrape, so that they might continue in office and carry the Reform question. . . . His intention was, to support Ministers right or wrong, rather than place them, at a moment like the present, under any necessity of abandoning the government of the country to the dominion of the Tories." In this truly astonish ing outburst, one is at a loss whether to admire more the absence of principle, of which the speaker boasts, or the absence of shame, with which he boasts of it.—The loan in question was one of ninety millions of florins, contracted by Russia at the time of the battle of Waterloo, one-third of which had been taken over by England, and one third by Holland, as the price of Russian support to the arrangement by which Flanders was annexed to Holland. Now that arrangement was terminated, by the establishment of the Belgian kingdom, Holland repudiated her share of the obligation, and England had to undertake the whole.—For Jones, see No. III.; for Wellesley Pole, No. XV.; and for the connection of Hume with Greek finance, Part I., No. VI.

This was the first piece contributed by Praed to the *Morning Post*, and in its columns appeared all the subsequent poems, except where it is otherwise specified.]

"Te sequar, O Graiæ gentis decus."—LUCR.

I MUST confess I like the plan
    Which Joseph Hume has taught,
For saving to an honest man
    The toil and time of thought.
I used to have a foolish way
    Of doing what was right;
But now, I'm all for Brougham and Grey;
    I'll vote that black is white.

That Russian Loan, in proper place,
    I own a sad *faux pas;*
In spite of Palmerston's grimace,
    In spite of Denman's law.
But why should either fret and fume,
    Smooth Lord or learned Knight?

It's wasting words.   I'll follow Hume,
   I'll vote that black is white.

When Goulburn talks, to make a shine,
   Of income falling off,
Sometimes I go away to dine,
   Sometimes I stay to cough.
Let dear Lord Althorp fructify
   To Thomson's great delight ;
I'll keep my Cocker in my eye,
   I'll vote that black is white.

The Whigs may move in Parliament
   That Jones has filled Gazettes,
That Grecian scrip pays ten per cent.,
   Or Wellesley Pole his debts ;
That all O'Connell says is true,
   That good is bad, day night ;
Move what they will, I'll help them through
   I'll vote that black is white.

If Plenty leaves our land to-day,
   I'll say she comes in showers ;
If we fall down to Gallia's sway,
   I'll swear she bends to ours ;
If heavy taxes gall you, sir,
   I'll prove to you they're light ;

And if you blame the minister,
   I'll vote that black is white.

I know that Joseph's full of fear,
   I'll vote that he is brave;
I know his fame's not very clear,
   I'll vote he is no knave;
I know that Joseph is a quack,
   I'll vote he's Solon, quite;
In short, I know that black is black,
   I'll vote that black is white.

XVIII.

LONG AGO.

[This appeared in the *Morning Post*, 10th August, 1832, prefaced by a reprint of the Author's own song, with the same refrain, for which see his Poetical Works, vol. II., p. 378.—Sir John Cam Hobhouse had now succeeded to a baronetcy, and was appointed Secretary at War in February 1832, in the place of Sir Henry Parnell, who had been removed from office for repeated acts of party insubordination.—The Crown and Anchor Tavern, in the Strand, was the head-quarters of the National Political Union. The author's burlesque introduction is subjoined.]

To the Editor of the " Morning Post."

SIR,—The sentimental song of which I send you a copy has just been published by Mr. Chappell. The author of it has most impudently, and without any acknowledgment, adapted to his own purposes the words of an affectionate effusion which I poured forth some months ago upon occasion of the triumphant exaltation of one of my fellow-radicals to those honours and emoluments to which we all aspire.

I beg you to insert the original stanzas, and to aid me in the exposure of the plagiary. My servile imitator may have the applause of the boarding-school, but justice will be done me at the Free-and-Easy.

I am, Sir, your obedient servant,

A WESTMINSTER ELECTOR.

"We were children together! Oh, brighter than mine," etc.

WE were patriots together ; Oh, placeman and peer
    Are the patrons who smile on your labours to-day ;
And Lords of the Treasury lustily cheer
    Whatever you do, and whatever you say.
Go, pocket, my Hobhouse, as much as you will ;
    The times are much altered, we very well know ;
But will you not, will you not, *talk* to us still,
    As you talked to us once, long ago, long ago ?

We were patriots together ! I know you will think,
    Of the cobblers' caresses, the coal-heavers' cries,
Of the stones that we threw, and the toasts that we
    drink,
Of our pamphlets and pledges, our libels and lies !
When Truth shall awake, and the country and town
    Be heartily weary of Althorp and Co.,
My Hobhouse, come back to the Anchor and Crown,
    Let us be what we were long ago—long ago !

XIX.

PLUS DE POLITIQUE.

[Appeared 13th August, 1832.—The third Reform Bill received the Royal Assent, 7th June, 1832.—For the riot at Derby see No. VI. That at Bristol was still more serious; in fact it was the only very serious riot that has disgraced English municipal annals for a century.—Dr. Coplestone (see Part I., No. XIV.) was now Bishop of Llandaff and Dean of St. Paul's.—The great cause of Small *v*. Attwood—a dispute over a contract for the sale of iron mines, was tried before Lord Lyndhurst, and occupied him all the winter of 1831-2. In November 1832, he delivered a celebrated judgment, which was however reversed six years later, on appeal. It is a leading case on the subject of fraud.—Mr. Isaac Pocock, the dramatizer of Walter Scott's novels, supplied the theatres with Operatic Dramas for twenty years. *The Miller and his Men, The Maid and Magpie, Rob Roy McGregor,* and *Hit or Miss,* are among the best known.—Three inferior stanzas, possibly by another hand, with which this piece concluded, were rejected by the author on reprinting it.]

"Je n' en parlerai plus."—DE BÉRANGER.

No politics! I cannot bear
To tell our ancient fame;
No politics! I do not dare
To paint our present shame.

What we have been, what we must be,
    Let other minstrels say;
It is too dark a theme for me:
    No politics to-day!

I loved to see the captive's chain
    By British hands burst through;
I loved to sing the fields of Spain,
    The war of Waterloo,
But now the Russian's greedy swords
    Are edged with English pay;
We help—we hire the robber hordes:
    No politics to-day!

I used to look on many a home
    Of industry and art;
I gazed on pleasure's gorgeous dome,
    On labour's busy mart:
From Derby's rows, from Bristol's fires,
    I turn with tears away;
I can't admire what Brougham admires:
    No politics to-day!

I've often heard the faithless French
    Denounced by William Pitt;
I've watched the flash, from this same bench,
    Of Canning's polished wit;

And when your Woods and Waithmans brawl,
　Your Humes and Harveys bray—
Good Lord! I'm weary of them all!
　No politics to-day!

Let's talk of Coplestone and prayers,
　Of Kitchiner and pies,
Of Lady Sophonisba's airs,
　Of Lady Susan's eyes;
Let's talk of Mr. Attwood's cause,
　Of Mr. Pocock's play—
Of fiddles—bubbles—rattles—straws!
　No politics to-day!

XX.

THE MAGIC BENCH.

[September 5th, 1832.—The statesmen here satirized are Lord Althorp, Sir James Graham, Sir John Cam Hobhouse, and Lord John Russell.—Lord Althorp had spoken several times in February 1830 on the subject of distress in the country, and in advocacy of retrenchment.—Sir James Graham, after his failure in the debate of March 1831, somewhat surprised his colleagues by his silence. A bitter complaint was made by Lord Brougham, of him and Mr. Charles Grant, on this account, in a private letter to Lord Grey.—Sir J. C. Hobhouse was unlucky in holding office as Secretary at War, after speaking and voting against flogging in the army. But it was due to him that an enquiry was instituted in the case of William Somerville, a bad business.—Lord John Russell published in 1823 an Essay on the History of the English Government and Institutions, in which he defended (with some reservations) the existence of anomalies in the Representative System, and wrote with veneration of Borough Charters.]

I HAVE heard of a lamp, whose virtue makes
Pearls of pebbles, and lawns of lakes ;
I have heard of a wand, whose mystic gold
Turns lovely to loathsome, young to old ;
But there is a Bench, of power to change
Far more rapid, and far more strange,

Than ever was given to mortal hand
By the mightiest charms of Fairyland.

A dull lord breathed a bitter curse
On the knaves that were robbing the public purse;
For nobody now, he was bold to declare,
In castle or cot, had a guinea to spare;
And the debt and the taxes made him fear
That the nation would all be starved next year.
But he sits on the Bench, and people say
He has flung five millions of money away.

A Baronet came from the far far North,
And he poured huge rivers of rhetoric forth,
Prating of fetters, and prating of thrones,
With serious looks, and solemn tones;
And quoting bits of Latin lore
To make the country members roar.
But he sits on the Bench, and he's as dumb
As an unstrung lute, or a broken drum.

A little man with a hooked nose came;
His voice was thunder, his glance was flame;
He said he had seen, and he heaved a sigh,
A hero flogged who was six feet high;

And he thought it a horrid, heathenish plan,
To punish the faults of so tall a man.
But he sits on the Bench, and the drummers vow
He carries a " cat " in his pocket now.

I saw a wise Lord John, who took,
Wherever he went, a learned book ;
It treated of Commons, it treated of Crown,
Of building up, and of pulling down ;
All cried who could—or could not—read,
The book was a charming book indeed.
But he sits on the Bench, and it's quite absurd,
He has eaten the volume every word.

Many I see who, years ago,
Were as white and fair as the new fallen snow ;
But they sit on the Bench, and lo ! they're black
As the plumage on the raven's back ;
And many whom we measured then,
Were found to be enormous men ;
But they sit on the Bench, and it's pretty well
    known
How very little they all are grown.

Would'st thou go thither ?   Oh study well
How thou may'st break the perilous spell !

Heed not a threat, and hear not a gibe;
Shun no labour, and touch no bribe:
Let the bright dame Honour be
Ever a guard and a guide to thee;
Love not the traitors, and trust not the French;
And so be safe on the Magic Bench!

XXI.
PLEDGES.

BY A TEN-POUND HOUSEHOLDER.

[Preparations were now being made for the General Election, which followed on the passing of the Reform Bill. This appeared on the 7th September, 1832. The Political Unions made a strenuous attempt to introduce the system of delegacy, in place of representation, by exacting pledges upon questions which were prominent at the moment. See especially the resolutions adopted at a meeting of the City of London Livery, *Ann. Reg.* LXXIV. 300.]

When a gentleman comes
With his trumpets and drums,
And hangs out a flag at the Dragon,
Some pledges, no doubt,
We must get him to spout
To the shop-keepers, out of a wagon.

For although an M.P.
May be wiser than we
Till the House is dissolved, in December,
Thenceforth, we're assured,
Since Reform is secured,
We'll be wiser by far than our member.

A pledge must be had
That, since times are so bad,
He'll prepare a long speech, to improve them;
And since taxes, at best,
Are a very poor jest,
He'll take infinite pains to remove them.

He must promise and vow
That he'll never allow
A Bishop to ride in his carriage;
That he'll lighten our cares
By abolishing prayers,
And extinguishing baptism and marriage.

He must solemnly say
That he'll vote no more pay
To the troops, in their ugly red jackets;
And that none may complain
On the banks of the Seine,
He'll dismast all our ships, but the packets.

That the labourer's arm
May be stout on the farm,
That our commerce may wake from stagnation,
That our trades may revive,
And our looms look alive,
He'll be pledged to all free importation.

And that city and plain
  May recover again
From the squabbles of Pitts and of Foxes,
  He'll be pledged, amidst cheers,
  To demolish the Peers,
And give us the balls and the boxes.

  Some questions our wit
  May have chanced to omit;
So, for fear he should happen to stumble,
  He must promise to go
  With Hume, Harvey, and Co.,
And be their obedient and humble.

  We must bind him, poor man,
  To obey their divan,
However their worships may task him,
  To swallow their lies
  Without any surprise,
And to vote black is white, when they ask him.

  These hints I shall lay,
  In a forcible way,
Before an intelligent quorum,
  Who meet to debate
  Upon matters of State,
To-night, at the National Forum.

XXII.

HUME TRANSLATED.

[25th September, 1832.—In October 1831 the *Times* declared war on Joseph Hume. The energy with which it was written and administered caused it to be, from the time of the Reform Bill controversy, unquestionably the first of daily newspapers.— Although Hume's watchful criticism of the estimates has earned for him, since his death, a certain posthumous reputation, it cannot be said that he ever, while he lived, earned the general respect of Englishmen.]

" Oh Bottom, thou art changed! what do I see on thee?"
" Bless thee, Bottom, bless thee! thou art translated."
Midsummer Night's Dream.

THE cunning man has scowled on me
Who changes black to white;
There never came wizard from over the sea
More strong to blast and blight;
He breathes his spell in a dark dark den,
The Chancellor well knows where;
His servants are devils, his wand is a pen,
And his circle is Printing House Square.

Many a strange and quaint disguise
    The crafty conjuror wears;
Sometimes he mutters blasphemies,
    Sometimes he mumbles prayers;
And if he rides to burn a town
    On a galloping Broom to-day,
To-morrow he quakes from the sole to the crown
    Like a Friar of Orders Grey.

I once was fair; not Waithman's face
    Was a fairer face than mine,
Ere the sorcerer's eye had marred the grace
    Of the features so divine;
On my brow a few black drops he threw,
    And a few fierce words he said,
And lo—and lo—wherever I go
    I wear an ass's head!

My hands were once extremely clean,
    I was an honest man;
No purer patriot ever was seen
    In Freedom's glorious van.
He has withered my arm with a fearful charm;
    It was wrought in Greece, they say;
And folks look grave and call me a knave,
    In the public streets to-day.

I used to cast accounts so fast
    That they called me Cocker's son;
The Board of Trade was all aghast
    When I rose to *carry one;*
But since that seal on my fate was set,
    I'm as dull as dull can be;
I've quite forgot my tare and tret,
    And I've lost my Rule of Three.

A mighty man that juggler is,
    So gloomy and so grim;
You shall not find a task, I wis,
    Too difficult for him;
He can make Lord Althorp half a wit,
    Lord Morpeth not a bore,
And give Lord Palmerston hope to sit
    In the seat where he sat before.

Would you retain for a twelvemonth's space
    The self-same hue and shape?
Would you shun to change your natural face
    For the face of an owl or ape?
Would you pray, through life's uncertain span.
    The fame you win to wear?
Avoid, if you can, the cunning man,
    Whose circle is Printing House Square!

XXIII.

THE OLD SOLDIER.

[13th October, 1832.—The campaign against the Dutch, to turn them out of Antwerp, undertaken by the French, while the English blockaded the port, was an odious necessity. My father, a Captain in the Navy, used to speak of the disgust with which his men, in H.M.S. Rover, regarded their mission to capture Dutch merchantmen in the Channel. All the prizes were given back, after Antwerp surrendered.]

I saw to-day an ancient man,
    An ancient man and poor ;
And he was sitting with his can
    Before his cottage door.
Right kindly he made room for me
    Upon the oaken bench,
And "Here's Old England's health" quoth he,
    "And sorrow take the French !"

"Good friend," said I, "you're vastly wrong,
    Your wits are all awry ;
Mounseer, whom we abused so long,
    Is now our best ally."

He laughed outright in merry glee,
    And, winking to his wench,
"Why, how his honour jests," quoth he,
    "To say so of the French !"

"In sooth it is a sober tale ;"
    So I to him replied :
"Together now our navies sail,
    Our troops charge side by side."
He stroked his head, which I might see
    Long years began to blench ;
"It's hard to swallow, Sir," quoth he,
    "Such stories of the French."

"Nay, comrade, it were really best
    To let these errors sleep ;
French patties are superbly drest,
    French wine is very cheap."
He sipped his grog ; could better be
    A soldier's thirst to quench ?
"Unwholesome is the mess," quoth he,
    "Whene'er the cook is French !"

"All this," I cried, "is idle cant;
    To-day new lights advance ;
Lord Palmerston and Mr. Grant
    Can find no fault with France."

He knocked his pipe against his knee,
    The ashes made a stench;
And, "Sir, there was a time," quoth he,
    "They both disliked the French."

I gave it up: 'twas all in vain:
    The veteran had his way;
He talked of Portugal and Spain,
    Of Marmont and of Ney;
He talked of tempests on the sea,
    Of grape shot in the trench;
"God bless the Duke!" so ended he;
    "How he did beat the French!"

XXIV.
A CABINET CAROL.

[18th October, 1832.—Lord Palmerston's disregard of mere party politics, though it was not, in him, the mark of any very exalted standard of political virtue, tended in the long run to win for him the confidence of Englishmen generally. But it exposed him to a good deal of obloquy, some of which was merited. The seat for Cambridge University, which he held in 1826 (see Part I., No. XIX.), he lost again at the General Elections of 1831; and he was now a candidate for the representation of Penryn and Falmouth.—The war Lord Howick is represented as condemning was not the Dutch war, but the great war with France, which kept his father for so many years in Opposition.]

"The statesman shews little practical wisdom, who obstinately adheres to his old opinions, when the circumstances which justified them exist no longer."—*Speech of Lord Palmerston.*

THERE was a time when I could sit
By Londonderry's side,
And laugh with Peel at Canning's wit,
And hint to Hume he lied;
Henceforth I run a different race,
Another soil I plough,
And though I still have pay and place,
I'm not a Tory now.

I've put away my ancient awe
   For mitre and for crown ;
I've lost my fancy for the law
   Which keeps sedition down ;
I think that patriots have a right
   To make a little row ;
A town on fire's a pretty sight :
   I'm not a Tory now.

When Howick damns with bitter sneer
   The friends of that vile war,
I whisper into Grant's dull ear
   " How just his strictures are ! "
When Burdett storms about expense,
   A smile comes o'er my brow :
Sir Francis is a man of sense.
   I'm not a Tory now.

I learn to be extremely shy
   With all my early cons ;
I'm very cold at Trinity,
   And colder at St. John's ;
But then, my Falmouth friends adore
   My smile, and tone, and bow ;
Don't tell them what I was before—
   I'm not a Tory, now !

A CABINET CAROL.

I'm always pleased with Jeffrey's prose,
    And charmed with Little's rhymes;
I'm quite convinced the nation owes
    Its welfare to the *Times*.
When people write the K—— a fool,
    And call the Q—— a frow,
I'm philosophically cool;
    I'm not a Tory now.

If Harvey gets Brougham's seals and seat,
    My friend will Harvey be;
If Cobbett dines in Downing Street,
    He'll have my three times three;
If Hunt in Windsor Castle rules,
    I'll take a house at Slough;
Tories were always knaves and fools.
    I'm not a Tory, now!

XXV.

STANZAS.

BY A TEN POUNDER OBJECTED TO.

[23rd October, 1832.—The first Registration, under the Reform Bill, was proceeding.]

    Sanctarum inscitia legum.—Hor.

I'm quite amazed! Twelve months and more
 I've taken monstrous pains
To raise my friends from shore to shore,
 And make them break their chains;
And much I've plotted, much I've planned,
 With energy and skill,
And yet I cannot understand
 The clauses of the Bill.

The patriots in the papers wrote
 To say the fight was won;
Yet some maintain I have a vote,
 And some aver I've none;

And bless me! do whate'er I can,
   And ask where'er I will,
I never find a gentleman
   Who comprehends the Bill.

Attorney Fleece is very good
   At anything obscure;
If nonsense can be understood,
   He'll understand it, sure;
There's no man better at a lease,
   Or sharper at a will;
But bless your heart! Attorney Fleece
   Is bothered by the Bill!

At Greek or Latin, you may swear,
   The schoolmaster is quick;
They say he'll construe, I declare,
   Right through a wall of brick;
But he's been poring for a week,
   And may be poring still;
It's infinitely worse than Greek—
   He can't translate the Bill.

My landlord, old Sir Charles, was sent,
   In the most flattering way,
From Hocus Hall to Parliament
   To help Reform, and Grey.

He sat, Sir, for the nation's sake,
    Till sitting made him ill :
And then—'twas easier to make,
    Than to make out—the Bill.

At last, to set the matter right,
    Two counsellors came down ;
And each, to make our darkness light,
    Has brought a wig and gown.
But one says " yes," and t'other " no,"
    A—" black," B—" white," until
I don't think either seems to know.
    The meaning of the Bill.

They say Lord Brougham has power to teach
    All sorts of puzzling things,
From alphabets and parts of speech
    Down to the crimes of kings.
If yet, in pamphlets and reviews,
    He loves young minds to drill,
Some day, perhaps, he will diffuse
    Some knowledge of the Bill.

XXVI.
AN EPISTLE
FROM AN OLD ELECTIONEERER TO A YOUNG SECRETARY.

[30th November, 1832.—Mr. Edward Ellice, M.P. for Coventry, the Secretary to the Treasury, to Mr. Charles Wood, Lord Grey's private secretary.—Lord Palmerston's candidature for Penryn fell through, and a proposal to put him in nomination for Lambeth was not well received. Eventually he was returned for South Hants.—Van Speyk was a minor hero of the successful Dutch campaign against the Belgians.]

I'VE canvassed, dear Charles, since we parted,
Our friends in this beautiful town ;
But really, I'm quite broken-hearted
To find the good cause going down.
Some pestilent, profligate Tory
Has done all the mischief, no doubt;
The voters are all in one story ;
They ask what the war is about.

I tell them of Gatton and Sarum ;
I cut up the Bishops and Peers ;
I ring the old useful alarum
Of negroes and whips in their ears ;

I point out the manifold mercies
   We've had since Sir Robert went out:
They all put their hands on their purses
   And ask what the war is about.

When they drink my success at my dinners,
   I speak in an eloquent strain;
And then, sir, the weavers and spinners
   Cry "bravo!" and "bravo!" again;
But just in the midst of the cheering
   Some brute at the bottom will shout—
"We all of us want to be hearing
   What all this here war is about!"

Some come with inquisitive faces,
   Some come with inquisitive tones;
One grumbles—another grimaces—
   Here pamphlets are flying—there stones.
If I go to a market or masquing,
   If I'm one at a row or a rout,
Belles, butchers, all long to be asking—
   Ah me! what the war is about.

The Aldermen pause in their feeding
   To babble of dam and of dyke;
My Lady insists upon reading
   The lines in her book on Van Speyk

Sir Andrew jumps up to abuse me,
    In spite of his years and his gout,
And his little girl lisps, to amuse me,
    " Tell Ma what the war is about."

We'll carry poor Palmerston through, Charles,
    Whatever the country may say;
But his Lordship, between me and you, Charles,
    Behaves in a very odd way;
He's clever at jesting and joking,
    Which surely we might do without;
But he won't—it's extremely provoking—
    Explain what the war is about!

XXVII.

THE BEGGAR'S THANKS.

[February 15th, 1833.—The Tithe War in Ireland, which called loudly for settlement, was settled by a transfer of the actual payment from the tenant to the landlord, which proved entirely successful. But the Whig measure for reform of the Irish Establishment went further. It proposed the reduction of the overgrown episcopate, and the secularization of a portion of the Church endowments. This proposal, in the end, was the ruin of the Grey Ministry, by disgusting Mr. Stanley with his part as Irish Secretary, and eventually causing him, with others, to secede. Just at first it seems to have been viewed with a good deal of favour.]

"He was grateful for the plan, though he admitted he desired much more."—*Speech of Mr. O'Connell, K.C.*

HE mutters no threat, he points no gibe,
   He speaks in civil tone;
It's truly puzzling to describe
   How loyal he is grown.
He owes a debt—it's very sweet
   To have such debts to pay;
He owes his thanks to Downing Street—
   He's grateful to Lord Grey.

THE BEGGAR'S THANKS.

In you green isle it is averred
    That treason has been hot;
Some houses have been burnt, I heard,
    And some old parsons shot.
But bless my heart! I'm quite prepared
    To hope a fairer day;
The great O'Connell has declared
    He's grateful to Lord Grey!

He always rises to protest
    If people prate of law;
A statute is to him a jest,
    An oath a wisp of straw.
Oh surely 'tis a charming plan,
    Whatever bigots say,
Which makes so excellent a man
    So grateful to Lord Grey!

Go on, my lords and gentlemen!
    Pull down what yet remains;
Drive to the Holy Pontiff's pen
    His flock of Bourkes and Shanes;
In honest men you'll hear and see
    Some anger, some dismay;
But Daniel and his friends will be
    More grateful to Lord Grey.

XXVIII.

A NURSERY SONG.

[February 19th, 1833. In a debate on sinecure places, Hume asked what service had Lord Frederick FitzClarence seen, that he should be rewarded with the Lieutenancy of the Tower. Some member said, "Waterloo." "I had forgot Waterloo," said Hume, amid laughter; "but was the noble lord there?" The answer was "Yes."]

"I had forgot Waterloo."—JOSEPH HUME.

Hume has been dotting and carrying one,
Hume has been helping O'Connell and son,
Hume has been proving that wrong is right,
Hume has been voting that black is white;
Hume has so many things to do,
Hume has forgotten Waterloo.

Hume has been studying tare and tret,
Hume has been summing the national debt,
Hume has been babbling of silk and grain,
Hume has been poring o'er Cocker and Paine,

A NURSERY SONG.

Hume is a sage and a patriot too—
Hume has forgotten Waterloo.

Hume has been jobbing with infinite skill,
Hume has been treating the poor Greeks ill,
Hume has been rivalling Bowring's crimes,
Hume has been chid in the fierce old *Times*,
Hume has been reading the Yellow and Blue—
Hume has forgotten Waterloo.

Hume for his toils has a wide wide scope;
Hume is a friend to the friends of the Pope,
Hume has a pleasure in Antwerp's fall,
Hume has an eye on Greece and Gaul,
Hume has a heart for a Quaker or Jew—
Hume has forgotten Waterloo.

Hume has been praising Bentham's schemes,
Hume has been puffing Thomson's dreams,
Hume has been hinting that piety's cant,
Hume has been frightening good Charles Grant;
Hume is to me what he is to you;
Hume has forgotten Waterloo.

XXIX.

STANZAS

ON SEEING THE SPEAKER ASLEEP IN HIS CHAIR, DURING ONE OF THE DEBATES OF THE FIRST REFORMED PARLIAMENT.

[These lines appeared on the 6th March, 1833. Messrs. Finn, Grattan, and Baldwin were members of O'Connell's "tail;" Mr. John Fielden was M.P. for Oldham.—The allusion to Cobbett produced a very clever skit, of which it was taken as the text, in which the idea was worked out at great length. See the *Morning Post* for 1st April. It began—

> "Mr. Cobbett asked leave to bring in, very soon,
> A Bill to abolish the Sun and the Moon.
> The honourable member proceeded to state
> Some arguments used in a former debate," etc, etc.

The authorship was not disclosed. Besides the heavenly luminaries, rain, wind, and the whole course of nature are to be reformed. Parliament is to

> " Provide for the World a more just Legislature,
> And impose an agrarian law upon Nature!"

The Wood of whom Lord Palmerston may have had a mean opinion in 1827 was not, of course, Charles, afterwards Lord Halifax, but the Alderman, Lord Hatherley's father, Queen Caroline's host.]

ON SEEING THE SPEAKER ASLEEP.

SLEEP, Mr. Speaker; it's surely fair,
If you don't in your bed, that you should in your chair;
Longer and longer still they grow,
Tory and Radical, Aye and No;
Talking by night, and talking by day;
Sleep, Mr. Speaker; sleep, sleep while you may!

Sleep, Mr. Speaker; slumber lies
Light and brief on a Speaker's eyes.
Fielden or Finn, in a minute or two,
Some disorderly thing will do;
Riot will chase repose away;
Sleep, Mr. Speaker; sleep, sleep while you may.

Sleep, Mr. Speaker; Cobbett will soon
Move to abolish the sun and moon;
Hume, no doubt, will be taking the sense
Of the House on a saving of thirteen pence;
Grattan will growl, or Baldwin bray;
Sleep, Mr. Speaker; sleep, sleep while you may.

Sleep, Mr. Speaker; dream of the time
When loyalty was not quite a crime,
When Grant was a pupil in Canning's school,
And Palmerston fancied Wood a fool.

Lord, how principles pass away!
Sleep, Mr. Speaker; sleep, sleep while you may.

Sleep, Mr. Speaker; sweet to men
Is the sleep that comes but now and then;
Sweet to the sorrowful, sweet to the ill,
Sweet to the children who work in a mill.
You have more need of sleep than they;
Sleep, Mr. Speaker; sleep, sleep while you may.

XXX.

PATRIOT AND PLACEMAN.

A NEW SONG, INSCRIBED TO THE ELECTORS OF
WESTMINSTER.

[6th May, 1833.—In April Mr. Stanley was promoted from the Irish Secretaryship to the Colonial Office, and his former place was accepted by Sir J. C. Hobhouse, who had retained his seat for Westminster at the General Election of 1832, though not without opposition, due to the attempts of the Unions to extort pledges. (See No. XXI.). Hobhouse manfully resisted this, but at the same time gave the strongest assurance of opposition to the assessed taxes, as then levied. The third Budget of Lord Althorp and Mr. Thomson incurred serious objection, because it did not deal with this question. Hobhouse, finding his position in the ministry untenable, resigned office; and being unwilling to oppose the Liberal Ministry, which was in danger of defeat, resigned also his seat for Westminster, with a view to re-election. He was immediately opposed by the Political Union, who chose Colonel Evans, afterwards Sir De Lacy Evans, as their candidate.

SIR JOHN was a patriot, who talked to the town
In a very fine style at the Anchor and Crown;

Sir John was a placeman, who went to entrench
His wisdom and wit on the Treasury Bench.
                            Derry Down.

Sir John was a patriot, all stutter and storm,
Who promised the people a ton of Reform !
Sir John was a placeman, who thought it would do
To give the poor people a bushel or two.
                            Derry Down.

Sir John was a patriot, whose scorn was immense
For the vermin who plundered the poor of their
    pence ;
Sir John was a placeman, who whispered a wish
To honest Lord Grey for a loaf and a fish.
                            Derry Down.

Sir John was a patriot, who used to exclaim
That flogging tall men was a horrible shame ;
Sir John was a placeman, who handled a whip,
And softly requested the privates to strip.
                            Derry Down.

Sir John was a patriot, who swooned when he saw
A soldier called out in support of the law ;
Sir John was a placeman, who sent, I declare,
The Colonels and Captains to Cork and to Clare.
                            Derry Down.

Sir John was a patriot, who valiantly swore
My windows and house should pay taxes no more;
Sir John was a placeman, who fled like a mouse,
When Althorp was taxing my window and house.
Derry Down.

Sir John was a patriot, who happened one day
To creep from his seat and his office away;
Sir John was a placeman, who laboured in vain
To creep to his seat and his office again!
Derry Down.

XXXI.

WHISTLE.

INTENDED TO BE SUNG BY SIR JOHN CAM HOBHOUSE,
AFTER HIS RE-ELECTION FOR WESTMINSTER.

[The Westminster nomination was on May 7th; and this appeared on the 8th.—Sir John could not obtain a hearing, and was pelted from the hustings.—Mr. Wakley had taken the lead in heckling him at the preceding election.—"Joseph" is Hume; he moved a resolution in the House against flogging in the army; Mr. Grote at this time was chiefly known as the mover of the Ballot Bill. Alderman Sir John Key had been Lord Mayor on the occasion of the banquet celebrated in No. XVI., and had moved the resolution against the House and Window Taxes.

This piece was not reproduced in the edition privately printed in 1835; but Praed writes, 26th May, 1833, "'Patriot and Placeman' was mine, as well as 'Whistle;' and it was generally held the more indisputably mine of the two."]

Oh whistle, and I'll come to you, Lord Grey;
Whistle, and I'll come to you, Lord Grey;
Whatever you do, and whatever you say,
Oh whistle, and I'll come to you, Lord Grey!

I promise, of course, what I promised before;
I speak as I spoke, and I swear as I swore;

But honest Lord Althorp to-morrow shall see,
A promise is pie-crust to Burdett and me.

 So whistle, and I'll come to you, Lord Grey;
 Whistle, and I'll come to you, Lord Grey;
 Whate'er be the pledges I swallow to-day,
 Just whistle, and I'll come to you, Lord Grey.

Perhaps I must talk, as I've talked long enough,
Of taxes, and ballot, and flogging, and stuff;
But Joseph, and Grote, and wise Alderman Key,
You know, will have little assistance from me.

 So whistle, and I'll come to you, Lord Grey;
 Whistle, and I'll come to you, Lord Grey;
 I'm a popular man, and I talk for display,
 But whistle, and I'll come to you, Lord Grey.

It's a terrible bore when the Radicals bring
Addresses, Petitions, and that sort of thing;
But a shake of the head, and a bend of the knee,
Is all they will get, if they bring them to me.

 Then whistle, and I'll come to you, Lord Grey;
 Whistle, and I'll come to you, Lord Grey;
 Just wait till I've sent Mr. Wakley away,
 Then whistle, and I'll come to you, Lord Grey.

Though vanished and lost are the praises you won,
Though I see you abused in the *Times* and the *Sun*,
Though they laugh, my dear lord, at your Family Tree,
These things are of little importance to me.

    So whistle, and I'll come to you, Lord Grey;
    Whistle, and I'll come to you, Lord Grey;
    As long as you've places, as long as you've pay,
    Oh whistle, and I'll come to you, Lord Grey!

XXXII.

THE ADIEUS OF WESTMINSTER.

[13th May, 1833. Colonel Evans was returned by a large majority, and Hobhouse, though he returned afterwards to public life, and to office, and was eventually raised to the Peerage as Lord Broughton, disappeared thenceforward from the front rank of rising statesmen.—"Old Glory" is Sir Francis Burdett, the aristocratically-minded squire who modelled his political career on that of Jack Wilkes, and kept his seat for Westminster many years, on the strength of his having done and said things, in his heyday of youth, which rendered him "impossible" as an office holder. Charles Fox, Sheridan, and Sir Samuel Romilly were all returned as M.P. for Westminster on one or more occasions; Capt. Sir Murray Maxwell was defeated by Romilly in 1818; and Mr. G. Lamb, in 1819, by Hobhouse and Sir Francis Burdett.— "Tram" is a kind of silk thread, originally imported from Italy, which turned up in the Budget debate.—Mr. Robert Grant was an advocate of the Abolition of Slavery in the Colonies, a question which, since Brougham's exposure of the judicial murder of the missionary Smith in Demerara (1829), had become urgent.—Sir John Campbell had lately been appointed Solicitor-General.— "*Qui tam*" were the first words, after the heading, in the old ex-officio informations for libel.]

WHEN first you came courting, John Cam, John Cam,
When first you came courting, John Cam,

You came with Old Glory,
Who hated a Tory
As much as a Hebrew hates ham, ham,
As much as a Hebrew hates ham.

Oh, then you were charming, John Cam, John Cam,
Oh, then you were charming, John Cam;
    As noisy and merry
    As Charley and Sherry,
And almost as wise as Sir Sam, Sam,
And almost as wise as Sir Sam.

Fine presents you brought me, John Cam, John Cam,
Fine presents you brought me, John Cam;
    A score of good reasons
    For tumults and treasons,
Imported *de chez Nôtre Dame, Dame,*
Imported *de chez Nôtre Dame.*

You prated and plotted, John Cam, John Cam,
You prated and plotted, John Cam;
    And at clubs played the knave,
    Till Rogers looked grave,
And gave you the title of Pam, Pam,
And gave you the title of Pam.

How oft on my hustings, John Cam, John Cam,
How oft on my hustings, John Cam,
    You preached Revolution
    With grand elocution,
Which maddened me just like a dram, dram,
Which maddened me just like a dram.

And that was your triumph, John Cam, John Cam,
And that was your triumph, John Cam;
    When I kicked up a row,
    You made a low bow,
Which in Turkey they call a salaam,—laam,
Which in Turkey they call a salaam.

You smiled approbation, John Cam, John Cam,
You smiled approbation, John Cam,
    When I cudgelled their backs well
    Who voted for Maxwell,
And flung filthy turnips at Lamb, Lamb,
And flung filthy turnips at Lamb.

And great were your praises, John Cam, John Cam,
And great were your praises, John Cam;
    And the trumpet of fame
    Blew Hobhouse's name
As far as Seringapatam,—tam,
As far as Seringapatam.

Ah! why did you ever, John Cam, John Cam,
Ah! why did you ever, John Cam,
    Get into disgrace,
    By taking a place,
And proving your principles sham, sham,
And proving your principles sham?

Go back to your cronies, John Cam, John Cam,
Go back to your cronies, John Cam;
    To Althorp, so funny
    In matters of money,
And Thomson, who tattles of tram, tram,
And Thomson, who tattles of tram.

To Grant, the religious, John Cam, John Cam,
To Grant, the religious, John Cam,
    Whose soul it annoys,
    That the little black boys
Should work for their cocoa and yam, yam,
Should work for their cocoa and yam;

To Russell the rhymer, John Cam, John Cam,
To Russell the rhymer, John Cam;
    To Graham, who stutters
    Of frigates and cutters,
And Campbell the Prince of *Qui Tam, Tam,*
And Campbell the Prince of *Qui Tam.*

We're parted for ever, John Cam, John Cam,
We're parted for ever, John Cam ;
   You can't think—oh heavens!
   With tall Colonel Evans—
You can't think how happy I am, am,
You can't think how happy I am!

XXXIII.

THIRTY-TWO AND THIRTY-THREE.

[22nd May, 1833. On the 13th a mass meeting had been called in Cold Bath Fields " to form a National Convention," with a view to protest against the Assessed Taxes, and other grievances. James Lee proposed "that Mr. Mee should take the chair." The meeting was then dispersed by the police, one of whom was murdered with a stiletto. The Coroner's jury found a verdict of Justifiable Homicide, which was afterwards quashed in the Court of King's Bench, as being flagrantly against the weight of evidence. But the murderer was acquitted by a jury.—Lord Milton, eldest son of Lord Fitzwilliam, was squibbed by Praed soon after, in consequence of a curious error in the new edition of the " Peerage " for 1834, by which, having succeeded to his father's title, he was given the additional step of a Marquisate, with the title of Rockingham. See the leading article in the *Morning Post* of 27th December, 1833 :—

> " Is he the Marquis, or is he the Earl?
> Wears he the Strawberry? wears he the Pearl?
> Is he the Milton we used to know
> In the House of Commons long ago—
> He that exalted on high his horn,
> And talked of taxes, and talked of corn,
> Till the Speaker wished he had never been born?
> The Milton that sat at our Ministers' backs?
> The Milton that swore he would pay no tax?"]

"Nous avons changé tout cela."—MOLIÈRE.

I often think it's very strange
    That people are so very slow
In finding out how all things change
    Which mortals think, or feel, or know.
What fools have done, they still will do;
    What fools have been, they still will be;
As if the world of thirty-two
    Had been the world of thirty-three.

When wise Lord Milton fiercely screamed
    " No taxes till the Bill is law,"
To all the Whigs Lord Milton seemed
    The noblest lord they ever saw :
At Michaelmas, if I and you
    Should plead, my friends, Lord Milton's plea,
As he was puffed in thirty-two
    We sha'n't be puffed in thirty-three.

Where patriots met a year ago
    To wave their hats, and strain their throats,
Lord Althorp took his pen, you know,
    And wrote them vastly civil notes;
But bless us, if a chosen few
    Are found admiring Lee and Mee,
They feel the thanks of thirty-two
    Are turned to thumps in thirty-three.

Of old, when long petitions came
   From Tom and Dick, who brew and bake,
We used to hear the Press proclaim
   That all the nation was awake.
If Dick and Tom, who bake and brew,
   To-day petition to be free,
"The nation" roared in thirty-two,
   It's just "the mob" in thirty-three.

Our Pyms and Hampdens made their bow
   To millions, or to myriads, then;
But Lord! they only babble now
   To half-a-score of drunken men.
Then, nothing into numbers grew;
   Now, numbers into nothing flee:
For one was ten in thirty-two,
   And ten are one in thirty-three.

What fairy with her liquid song—
   What sorcerer with his mystic spell
Turns wrong to right, and right to wrong,
   And Hell to Heaven, and Heaven to Hell?
Brougham says—and what Brougham says, is true—
"Don't marvel at the things you see:
For we were Whigs in thirty-two,
   And we are Whigs in thirty-three!"

XXXIV.

THE WASHING OF THE BLACKAMOOR.

[24th May, 1833. "These verses," Praed wrote, "were licked into shape by me from a very rude sketch, by I know not whom." —Mr. Stanley, at the Colonial Office, found himself called on to settle the difficult question of the compensation to be granted for Slavery in the West Indies. His first proposal was for a loan of fifteen millions to the slave owners, to be repaid in some fashion by deductions from the wages of the slaves when free. Eventually the fifteen millions were increased to twenty, and the loan converted into a grant.—Sir T. Fowell Buxton succeeded Brougham as the leader of the Anti-Slavery party.—Dr. Lushington, afterwards the Dean of Arches, was a consistent Abolitionist.—The "youthful Tully" is Macaulay; the story how he tendered his resignation in July is well told in his biography by Sir George Trevelyan.— Lord Howick resigned his office, that of Under Secretary of State for the Colonies, on similar grounds with Macaulay, objecting to the intermediate apprenticeship, and opposing the resolutions in which Stanley embodied his plan.]

"Vivant qui nigra in candida vertunt."—Juv.

THERE was a little man,
And he had a little plan
To set the West Indies all right, O;

And quoth he, "The House I'll teach
In a pretty little speech,
How to wash the Blackamoor white, O."

There was a House wherein
Were Fielden, Faithfull, Finn,
And they listened with infinite delight, O,
When in Biblical quotation
He breathed his expectation
Of washing the Blackamoor white, O.

There was a grave philosopher
Who vowed the plan to toss over,
Which seemed all his visions to blight, O;
Fowell Buxton was his name,
And he muttered "Fie for shame!
This won't wash the Blackamoor white, O."

There was Lushington, the Doctor,
That very learned Proctor
Who in speaking spits fire and spite, O;
He at this was discontented,
And to nothing less assented
Than washing the Blackamoor white, O.

There was a youthful Tully,
Determined not to sully
His laurels so green and so bright, O;
And he sighed, " With heartfelt sorrow
I must leave my place to-morrow,
If you won't wash the Blackamoor white, O."

There was a lord, sad-hearted
Since from office he departed,
And he rose in a melancholy plight, O,
To say that he had rather
Go himself and teach his father
How to wash the Blackamoor white, O.

There was a band which marched,
Four hundred, stiff and starched,
To Downing Street, to fight the good fight, O;
Saints, sinners, all came forth,
From the south and from the north,
All to wash the Blackamoor white, O.

There was a private room
Where they laboured to illume
Dark councils with sparks of new light, O;
And stunned the Administration
With excommunication,
If it wouldn't wash the Blackamoor white, O.

There was a mortgage deed,
    As fair a thing to read
As ever a lawyer could write, O;
    But the parchment, people say,
    Lighted fires for Brougham and Grey,
While they washed the Blackamoor white, O.

There was a merchant ship
    Returning from a trip,
And her owner was sad at the sight, O;
    Despairing of Barbadoes,
    For rum and muscovadoes,
After washing the Blackamoor white, O.

There was a hungry nation,
    Which heard with much vexation
That her ministers meant, if they might, O,
    To tack to that long debt of hers
    The price of Stanley's metaphors,
And of washing the Blackamoor white, O.

XXXV.

MR. LITTLETON'S FRIENDSHIP.

[4th June, 1833. In place of Sir John Cam Hobhouse, an Irish Secretary was, after some difficulty, found in Mr. Walhouse Littleton, M.P. for Staffordshire, who was married to a daughter of the Marquess Wellesley, now Viceroy, and gave dinner parties in Grosvenor Place. He made a mess of it, five times as great as that made by any other Englishman who has ever been Irish Secretary, one resulting in the total retirement of his chief, Earl Grey, from politics. He was then made a peer, with all decent precipitation, in May 1835.—Mr. Kennedy, a representative of Scottish interests in the Ministry, is memorable chiefly as having survived long enough to contradict Lord Brougham's accounts of transactions in which he was concerned.—Mr. Spring Rice, afterwards Lord Monteagle of Brandon, was now Secretary of the Treasury.—Dr. Doyle was the Catholic Archbishop of Dublin.]

"He proceeded to explain the motives which had led him most reluctantly to accept office; it was solely on public grounds, and to relieve the Ministry from the embarrassment in which they were then placed."
Report of Mr. Littleton's Speech.

Oh yes, the gentleman has place,
    The gentleman has pay;
His worth has found its proper grace
    With Althorp, Brougham, and Grey;

But don't suspect the patriot cares
    For any private ends ;
For—hear him—hear him—he declares
    It's all to serve his friends.

Pert Kennedy looks wondrous blue ;
    Spring Rice detests a mob ;
There's nobody disposed to do
    This pretty Irish job :
O'er all the Whigs in Downing Street,
    A sudden fate impends ;
Our member has a nice snug seat,
    Why mayn't he serve his friends ?

Alas, it is a weary toil
    To find a proper man
To break a lance with Doctor Doyle,
    To change a cuff with Dan !
A luckless life the man will lead
    Whom Grey to Dublin sends !
He would refuse—he would indeed—
    Except to serve his friends.

You see, in country and in town—
    I own it, if I must—
They're tearing Althorp's picture down,
    And breaking Russell's bust ;

When far and near there's hardly one
    Who likes them or defends,
How kind of Mr. Littleton
    To go and serve his friends!

We want the good to come to pass
    They promised us last year;
We want to see through cheaper glass,
    To swallow cheaper beer.
But never mind, our idle whim
    Our member's taste offends;
What are our little wants to him?
    He wants to serve his friends.

Some day, no doubt, they'll pay the debt
    Which they're incurring now;
Some day he'll wear a coronet
    Upon his lordly brow;
Though Radicals and Tories sneer,
    The country comprehends
That whenso'er he's made a Peer,
    'Twill be—to serve his friends.

XXXVI.

THE REMONSTRANCE.

[9th November, 1833. In the *Times* of October 28 is a report extracted from a Durham paper, describing how Mr. Attwood, M.P. for Birmingham, the President of the Northern Political Union, indignant at being ignored by the Committee who were preparing a banquet at Gateshead to Lord Durham, organized an open-air meeting, and prepared a long address of an unfriendly character to his lordship. Mr. Attwood and his friends got into the Hotel Committee room just before dinner-time, and tried to read the address through. Poor Lord Durham was reduced to claiming "the protection of the Committee."—Mr. Attwood's account appeared in other papers.—Mr. Hutt, M.P. for Hull, and Mr. W. H. Ord, M.P. for Newport, were among those who, as Praed writes in a note, "supported the noble Earl on this distressing occasion."

In this month Edward M. Fitzgerald put out a series of squibs in the *Morning Post*, which there is some difficulty in distinguishing from Praed's. They are: 16th November, *Not Guilty*; 18th, *The Midnight Cabinet*; 20th, *A Whig à la Ude*; 23rd, *Cadeaux from Calcutta*; 29th, *Thoughts on a lately Published Pamphlet* (this is known to be by Fitzgerald, on Praed's authority) ; December 13th, *Give me the Penny Cup!* January 1st, 1834, *Thirty-three and Thirty-four* (this Praed disclaimed). Of these, the first, second, sixth and seventh are close imitations of Praed's style, and the fourth and fifth of Thomas Moore's. Perhaps it was in connection with this circumstance that Praed, contrary to his usual custom, signed No. XXXVI., with a ≡].

"He added, in agitated but emphatic tones, 'Mr. Attwood, I have not deserved this from you!'"—See MR. ATTWOOD'S *account of the Skirmish at Gateshead.*

Mr. ATTWOOD—we're going to dinner;
    Mr. Attwood—the time, and the place!
Mr. Attwood—as I am a sinner,
    The thing is too long for a grace.
Ten columns! it's out of the question;
    Go out, Mr. Attwood, pray do;
You'll ruin his lordship's digestion!
    He has not deserved it of you!

The voice of the people, Heaven bless it,
    Is sweet to us all, as you know;
But, really sometimes, we confess it,
    It's terribly *mal-à-propos:*
To-morrow, no doubt, he'll be able
    To talk with you, many or few;
But just when the turtle's on table—
    He has not deserved it of you.

You see there are gentlemen present
    Who have come to our party from far;
Consider—it's vastly unpleasant—
    Consider how hungry they are!
From Newport and Hull they have posted,
    With speeches, and appetites too;
They came to be toasted, not roasted—
    He has not deserved it of you!

Last year, when your orators spouted,
    They spouted in rapture his fame;
Last year, when your multitudes shouted,
    They shouted in riot his name;
Last year you came up with caresses;
    Last year you were licking his shoe;
Away with your ill-bred addresses!
    He has not deserved it of you!

And surely you'll listen to reason!
    Who is it you come to put down?
The noblest of traders in treason,
    The first of the foes of the Crown;
The pilot who sits in the steerage
    With Faithfulls and Finns for his crew;
His lordship—the *Hunt* of the Peerage—
    He has not deserved it of you!

Oh never! Lord Durham has others
    To censure, to scorn, to condemn;
But you, his dear friends and sworn brothers,
    Should never take service with them.
The good may despise and detest him,
    The honest, the loyal, the true;
But why should the traitors molest him?
    He has not deserved it of you!

XXXVII.

THE RUSSELL MELODIES.

NO. I.

[11th November, 1833.—Mr. De Vear was the proposer of Sir J. C. Hobhouse at the Election.—"The Borough," in the talk of those days, was not Southwark, but Westminster.—Lord Durham, in his Gateshead speech, which contained a good deal of personal matter, set himself to reveal, as a matter of historical interest, that his father-in-law had, immediately after the formation of his Ministry, entrusted to him, personally, the preparation of the Reform Bill. In this task, he added, he had been "assisted with advice" by Lord John Russell, Sir James Graham, and Lord Duncannon.—Mr. Charles Wood was now Treasury Whip.

These pieces were accompanied with burlesque prefaces and notes by the author.]

" We have often been reproached for the unkindness of our allusions to Lord John Russell's poetical works. We confess we do think *Don Carlos* the worst tragedy extant, and we never found anybody of a different opinion, except one sallow gentleman who writes in the *Edinburgh Review*, and visits occasionally at Holland House. But we readily admit that many of his lordship's unpublished *jeux d'esprit* and *vers de société* possess merit ; and we are willing to make amends to the noble lord by presenting a few of them to the public. The affectionate pathos of the following stanzas, which were addressed to the late member for Westminster, on his retiring from place and parliament, has made them very popular in fashionable circles."

OH SNATCHED AWAY IN THY FIRST QUARTER.[1]

Oh snatched away in thy first quarter,[2]
We have for thee nor star nor garter;
But Grey and Brougham make jests about
Thy taking in and turning out,
And call thee, in the Cabinet, their Martyr.

And in the Borough, where our game [3]
Is all at sixes and at sevens,
De Vear, deep fellow, sings thy fame,[4]
And swears he'll move the earth, the heavens! [5]
As if there were a chance with Colonel Evans!

[1] *Note by Lord John Russell.*—I am indebted for the idea of these stanzas to one of the Hebrew Melodies. I mention it that the reader may see my melody is as much superior to Byron's, as my play was to Schiller's.

"Oh snatched away in Beauty's bloom," etc.

[2] *Note by Mr. Joseph Hume.*—Sir John appears to have held the Irish Secretaryship for thirty-three days. The salary of the office being £5,500 per annum, the baronet will be found to have earned £497 5s. 4½d. —errors excepted.

[3] *Note by Lord Althorp.*—This is a mistake. In many parts of the country, I must candidly confess, the late Act rendered game scarce. But in Westminster I may venture to assure my noble friend it can have done little harm, because, in point of fact, for many years there has been in Westminster no game at all. But His Majesty's Government will not oppose the appointment of a committee to inquire into the subject.

Note by Sir Francis Burdett.—It is no mistake at all.

[4] *Note by dear De Vear.*—I never sing.

[5] *Note by ditto.*—I never swear.

Away! We know we've lost our Hobby;
We know close seats exist no longer ;[1]
Will this console us in the lobby,
Or make Wood's list one vote the stronger?
And thou—who laughest at my vapours—
Thyself art packing up thy papers![2]

[1] *Note by the Duke of Bedford and Earl Fitz William.*—Pooh!
[2] *Note by Earl Durham.*—This apostrophe is addressed to me. The papers alluded to are the rough drafts of the Clauses of the Reform Bill, the preparation of which was entrusted to me by my noble father-in-law.

Note by Mr. Joseph Hume.--I suspect that Lord Durham's share in the Reform Bill will turn out a MONTE MUS.

XXXVIII.

THE RUSSELL MELODIES.

NO. II.

[13th November, 1833.—Mr. Manners Sutton was Speaker, and Mr. Bernal, as above noticed, Chairman of Committees.—The *Quarterly Reviewer* of Miss Burney's "Memoirs of Dr. Burney," was John Wilson Croker; his meritorious but not always well-guided zeal for accuracy in small matters of fact was said to be especially stimulated by the prospect of proving that a lady had understated her age. See Macaulay's Review of the Diary of Miss Burney (Madame D'Arblay), a book published ten years later.]

"We are happy to learn that our commencement of this series of papers has delighted, in no ordinary degree, the friends of the noble poet, to whose effusions we thus give a circulation which his own amiable diffidence would have denied them. "*Oh snatched away,*" has already been set to music by a distinguished amateur composer; and a certain secretary of State, residing not twenty miles from Carlton Gardens, has been heard to say that the *Russell Melodies* deserve a second reading much better than the Russell Bills. Encouraged by these circumstances, we present to our readers a second selection from the MSS. entrusted to us, a selection made, of course, in compliment to the not unnatural preference of the illustrious author, since it cannot be expected that we should sympathize in the exultation he expresses upon the event which is his theme."

ODE ON THE PASSING OF THE REFORM BILL.[1]

'Tis done! I have finished my monument now;
What tidings of transport for Sutton and Bernal!
Take the brass—all the brass—of the chancellor's brow,
You won't build a monument half so eternal.

'Tis as tall as a pyramid—wonderful edifice—
Though it threatens the stars—(see the book of Belzoni);
'Tis as tall as Lord Grey, though that classical head of his
Brushes down a nice *star*, now and then, for a crony.[2]

---

[1] *Note by Lord John Russell.*—As in my *Don Carlos* I imitated Schiller, and in my Reform Bill took a leaf from the Abbé Sièyes, I have, in the following stanzas, appropriated many ideas, without hesitation, from one of the Odes of old Horace. The Roman poet has been accused of vanity in the application of extravagant panegyric to his own works. If such an imputation is cast upon me, I answer briefly that, except by a poetical licence, I am not the author of the Reform Bill; it was framed by Lord Durham; Sir James Graham and Lord Duncannon were consulted by him on some important points. For my own part, I gave him advice upon nothing, except a trifling matter connected with the well-doing of the borough of Tavistock. I may venture to subjoin Horace's Ode, since, under the Reform Act, all country gentlemen understand Latin:—

"Exegi monumentum ære perennius," etc.

[2] *Note by —— —— Esq.*—I was in the Fifth Form at Eton with the First Lord of Treasury. I remember his making a pun about an often-quoted line—*Stellæ sponte suâ jussæne vagentur et errent.*—"The question don't admit of discussion," said he; "the Stars would be good for nothing without the Orders!"

It shall last, for the weal and the strength of the
    nation,
Unharmed by the changes of destiny's weather;
No flight of the times shall impair its foundation,[1]
    While Hume and the tides go on moving
    together.

And me, its wise author, the world shall remember,
    As long as a talkative mayor shall preside
At Guildhall, o'er the turtle and toasts, in November,
    With a mute Lady Mayoress perched by his side.

Of me they shall say on the banks of the Tweed,
    Of me they shall say on the banks of the
    Shannon,
" Lord John, whom we used to think little indeed,
    But who grew a great man by the help of Dun
    cannon,[2]

"To his praise be it told, was the first to bring over
    A new and original French Constitution,

---

[1] *Note by a poor Author.*—Horace did not live in the days of newspaper criticism, or he would not have been so bold as Lord John. A flight of the *Times* is a very serious thing.

[2] *Note by Lord Duncannon.*—England will understand, sooner or later, how much she owes *me*. Ostensibly, indeed, I am content to be, like the chaste Diana, *Silvarum potens*, First Commissioner of Woods and Forests; but I am more than meets the eye; " no waiter, but a Knight Templar ; " a Legislator in disguise—a Lycurgus under a domino. Lord Durham can explain this.

Importing the treasure from Calais to Dover
On board of His Majesty's ship *Revolution.*"

Oh crown me, Melpomene, nymph of sad numbers![1]
    Though over my play, if you ever begin it,
You slumber as sound as the President slumbers[2]
    At the Board of Control, o'er an eloquent minute,

Yet crown me with laurel; to-night at Old Drury
    You may look at a case like my own, if you will;
The play is but so-so; yet let me assure ye,
    You'll find some magnificent things in the *Bill!*

---

[1] *Note by the Quarterly Reviewer of Miss Burney's Memoirs.*—We have found in the Registry of the Parish of Parnassus, that this "nymph," the daughter of Thespis and Mnemosyne, was baptized B.C. 539; so that she was two thousand three hundred and seventy-two years old when this Ode was composed.

[2] *Note by one of the Commissioners of the Board of Control.*—The Rt. Hon. Charles Grant is a psychological curiosity. He is the drowsiest philosopher of his own or of any day. He writes in his sleep, reads in his sleep, eats in his sleep, drinks in his sleep. He sleeps at the Board, he sleeps in the house, he sleeps at Court, and he sleeps in the Cabinet. He sleeps while you talk to him, and he sleeps while he talks to you. He is the seven sages and the seven sleepers in his own proper person.

XXXIX.

THE RUSSELL MELODIES.

NO. III.

[20th January, 1834.—The Penny Cups, purchased by subscription in London, were presented to Lord Althorp, Lord Grey, and Lord John Russell. Fitzgerald's best piece, of those above-mentioned (see Note on No. XXXVI.), is an appeal from Lord Durham to Lord John, to make over the trophy to himself.—Lord Grey was now tired of office, and unwilling to meet Parliament again; but was persuaded to remain by a round robin from Ministers, which is printed in Lord Brougham's Memoirs.—The allusion in the prefatory remarks to Lord Althorp refers to his recent Bank Charter Act and speech on proposing it; by this measure the notes of the Bank of England were made a legal tender for amounts of five pounds and upward].

"We do not know by what negligence on our part it has happened that this interesting series has been so long discontinued. We were reminded of our error on Saturday by the circulation of the little effusion which we present to our readers to-day. It has been composed by the noble author on occasion of the expressed disposition of Lord Grey to escape from the fatigues of office; and we are assured that the strong paths with which it has been sung to the noble Lord by the various members of his family who are qualified to take part in it, has produced a wonderfully tranquillizing effect upon the Premier's mind. We do not flatter the author of *Don Carlos* too much, when we express our conviction that the present stay of Earl Grey in office is attributable not more to the favour of his Sovereign, or the cordiality of his colleagues, than to the seductive harmony of the *Russell Melodies*, No. III.

"We omit the variorum notes. The little poem is sufficiently intelligible without them, and their insertion would trench too much upon our space. Selection is an invidious task; if we take one note, we are forced to take as many as are brought to us. The Chancellor of the Exchequer denies this; but we think him wrong."

FLY NOT YET.

Fly not yet! We're all agreed
That office, like a noxious weed
Which nicer taste rejects, disdains,
Grows sweeter for its stings and stains
    To Goderich, Grant and Co.
'Twas but that we might hold it fast,
The Bill, the glorious Bill, was passed,
For whose fourscore immortal clauses
The people gave three penny vases;
    Oh stay! oh stay!
Whigs so often vainly long
For pay and place, that oh, 'twere wrong
    So soon to let them go.

Fly not yet! The thief that stood
Of yore beneath the fatal wood
Now tried the rope, now paced the cart,
But seemed unwilling to depart
    When the doomed hour was near;
And thus a Whig, much cuffed about,
Will often talk of "going out;"

Will hint he's done—will vow he'll do it,
But will not, till they drive him to it.
    Oh stay! oh stay!
When did Premier ere bring in
So many of his kith and kin,
    To serve their country here?

XL.
THE RUSSELL MELODIES.

NO. IV.

[25th January, 1834.—Compare No. XXIV., and Part III. No. III. Of the M.P.s mentioned in this piece Mr. James Halse was Praed's successful antagonist in the contested election of 1832. Mr. Ross was the Conservative Whip, and had been Praed's colleague in the representation of St. Germains. Maurice and Morgan O'Connell were both joints in their father's "tail."]

"In the Ode which we select for the fourth number of the *Russell Melodies*, the noble author imitates the spirited remonstrance addressed by Horace to the Roman coquette Barine. Horace complains that the adoration which is still offered to the false flirt, in spite of her repeated perfidies and perjuries, makes him doubt the existence of a retributive Providence. We think the noble author, in many recent examples of popular profligacy, has good grounds for questioning the existence of any sense of justice or feeling of decency, in the minds of those by whom praise or blame is in our times awarded to political character.

"Lord Palmerston is utterly unable to inform us to what noble lord his friend's stanzas are addressed."

ODE TO A NOBLE LORD.

IF you, my dear lord, had been ever the worse
For the profligate things you have done;
If the title you bear were a scoff and a curse
To the scribes of the *Times* and the *Sun*,

Perhaps I might learn, in your sorrow and shame,
    Whate'er the Rotunda might say,
To fancy consistency more than a name,
    And truth a good thing in its way.

But you—when you've babbled your jests and your gibes
    At all that you've lived by for years,
When you've shuddered at sinecures, shivered at bribes,
    And shaken your head at the Peers,
Go back to your seat amid shouts of applause
    In every possible tone,
And your principles seem to the friends of our cause
    As pure, I suspect, as my own.

It's a glory for you to be racking your brains
    In showing to Pease and to Pryme
That Englishmen used to wear infamous chains
    In Pitt's and in Percival's time;
In proving of taxes and proving of trade
    Whatever you used to deny,
And sneering at blunders by Castlereagh made
    Since he cannot get up to reply.

Bright Venus, you know, my lord, laughs from above
    At the sad things her votaries do;

And surely, the falsehoods we pardon in love
    May be pardoned in politics too;
For the ribbands—the garters love maddens to touch,
    Ambition as gracefully kneels,
And lovers don't long for their letters so much
    As ministers long for their seals!

Hail, light of the House! The new Parliament men
    Support you in all you have done;
The old, though they meant to be going at ten,
    Say "Aye" to your motion at one;
The well-studied trope, which with Calvert succeeds,
    As surely with Codrington thrives,
And the "Hear" is as loud from your Marshall of Leeds,
    As it is from your Halse of St. Ives.

When you say "Mr. Speaker," and stand on the floor,
    And wave your rhetorical wrist,
Poor Ross in despair hurries down to the door,
    And mournfully looks at his list;
At the sound of your voice, at the beam of your smile,
    The Big Beggarman is aghast;
Such wisdom, such wit, he's afraid, will beguile
    His Maurice and Morgan at last.

XLI.

THE RUSSELL MELODIES.

NO. V.

[8th March, 1834.—In introducing the Reform Bill, Lord John said, "He believed the *legitimate* influence of wealth and station would always remain, and that such legitimate influence was all that *should* remain."—The adventures of Sir John Campbell, the Solicitor-General, in search of a seat, are the theme of three of these pieces, which the author seems to have thought, in reviewing them, a disproportionate allowance. See Nos. L., LI.—On the 1st March Sir John accepted the Attorney-Generalship, which vacated his seat at Dudley. On the 4th he was defeated at the poll, his defeat being attended with a serious election riot. Morpeth and Tiverton were suggested for him; Malton fell to Sir C. C. Pepys, the new Solicitor-General. Campbell finally obtained a seat at Edinburgh].

"The Bill was not intended to destroy the legitimate influence of property."—*Speeches of Lord John Russell (passim).*

SIR JOHN to Dudley is gone away
With a confident tone, and a visage gay;
Sir John from Dudley is coming back,
With an altered tone, and a visage black;
The dolts at Dudley are very dense,
And deaf to "legitimate influence."

How shall we manage their fault to mend?
The Earl Fitzwilliam is my friend;
Though Wetherell scold, though Croker scoff,
We'll send the knight in his chariot off;
At Malton none are known to fence
Against " legitimate influence."

If Earl Fitzwilliam will not smile,
I have a colleague, Lord Carlisle;
He knows, I fancy, a thing or two
Of what the folk at Morpeth do;
They have a horror of pounds and pence,
But a taste for " legitimate influence."

If Lord Carlisle will not be won,
I am his Grace of Bedford's son;
Our own ten-pounders in the West
Will be happy to see their learned guest;
Tavistock men are men of sense;
They love " legitimate influence."

For true Reformers there will be
In Downing Street a jubilee,
When the champion proud of Freedom's cause
Shall come to manufacture laws,
Chosen—no matter how or whence—
M.P. for " legitimate influence."

XLII.

THE RUSSELL MELODIES.

NO. VI.

[19th March, 1834.—The Bishop of Chichester was Dr. Maltby. He was made comfortable by a translation to Durham, in 1836.— Lord Brougham was credited with a desire to break up the Ministry and extrude Lord Grey with a view to his own succession. At least, some utterances of his in the Court of Chancery, characteristic of his perpetual restlessness, were so construed.]

" The poem we present to our readers to-day, is one in which the noble author invites the First Lord of the Treasury to dinner, in a loose imitation of Horace's pretty Ode, ' Œli, vetusto nobilis ab Lamo.'
" We have formerly illustrated his lordship's adaptations from the classics by quotations from the originals. Some of our fair readers have been angry with us for this ; but their frowns would scarcely have moved us to substitute the clumsy English of Francis for the exquisite Latin of Horace, if a more reverend adviser had not supported their petition. The Bishop of Chichester assures us ' he cannot be comfortable without a *translation.*' "

Illustrious Premier ! noble Peer,[1]
Whose family will live in story,[2]

[1] " Œlius, whose ancient lineage springs,
  From Lamus," . . .
[2] " From whom the illustrious race arose," etc.

While yon Red Book from year to year
　Immortalizes Whig and Tory,

(Since in that wondrous book to-day
　We scarcely read of any others,
As touching power, or tasting pay,
　But Earl Grey's sons, and Earl Grey's brothers),

Next spring—if any part is true [1]
　Of what that arch wag, Brougham, is croaking
In his dark Court, of me and you,
　With malice that is quite provoking—

Next spring we must, alas! give o'er
　Our pretty plans, our pleasant places;
And hide, upon Life's weedy shore,[2]
　Our most uncomfortable faces.

Let us be merry, ere our sin
　By such rebuke is overtaken;

[1] "If the old shower-foretelling crow
　Croak not her boding note in vain."
[2] "To-morrow's eastern storm shall strew
　. . . . . with weeds the shore."

Bring Wood[1]—to tell us, with a grin,
    How vastly well we've saved our bacon;[2]

The Grants shall join us, half alive;[3]
    Tired Melbourne shall tie up his knocker;
And dear dim Althorp shall contrive
    To steal one afternoon from Cocker.

---

[1] "Then pile the wood while yet you may."
[2] "Feast upon the fatted swine."
[3] "Give to your slaves one idle day"

XLIII.

MAXIMS.

[We return to the 16th January, 1834, for the date o this piece. Lord Auckland was President of the Board of Trade, but he combined with this office the Mastership of the Mint, which had been the subject of a reform in 1831, whereby the Tories had diminished the salary from £3,000 to £2,000. It was, after all, little more than a dignified sinecure].

"Lord Auckland is understood to be appointed permanently on constitutional grounds."—*Globe*, January 14th.

If a Tory is ever found out
   In pocketing twenty pence,
The thing is a job, no doubt;
   It admits of no defence:
If a Whig has the luck to secure
   Some twenty thousand pounds,
It is all arranged, be sure,
   On "Constitutional grounds."

If a Tory dares distrust
   The faith of our fiercest foe,

Suspicion is quite unjust,
   And jealousy vastly low:
If a Whig with a bold blockade
   Our ancient friend confounds,
It is done for the good of trade,
   On "Constitutional grounds."

If a Tory punishes crimes
   In Kerry or in Clare,
The wisdom of the *Times*
   Proclaims it quite unfair:
If a Whig with a troop of horse
   The Murphys and Macs astounds,
He cuts and thrusts, of course,
   On " Constitutional grounds."

If a Tory gives a place
   To a nephew, or a son,
Good lack! a thing so base
   Was never, never done!
If a Whig with his countless kin
   The nation's purse surrounds,
They slip their fingers in
   On " Constitutional grounds."

Then take, my lord, oh take
   The gift the Greys provide,

For the Constitution's sake,
    And for no end beside;
And think, on quarter-day,
    Of the friend who thus expounds
The rights of place and pay,
    On " Constitutional grounds."

XLIV.

THE SONG OF THE NURSE.

EXTRACTED FROM THE FORTHCOMING EDITION OF "GAMMER GURTON'S GARLAND."

[6th February, 1834. If Lord Melbourne and Lord Duncannon at the time, and Sir George Grey and Sir Charles Wood at a subsequent date, may be considered to have justified the good fortune which partly befell them because they were connected with Earl Grey, the same can hardly be said of Lord Durham, Mr. Ellice, and the rest of the "tribe of fortune," for whose names the "Book of Dignities" and the Peerage may alternately be consulted. The fact was, Lord Grey emerged from an unofficial station, late in life, to be Premier of a ministry and leader of a party composed of untried men. He was of reserved habits, and could work best with the men he knew. A ring was early formed about him, and good things in plenty fell to the members of it. When they had been satisfied, other appointments were made with more regard to merit than had been usual before his time.]

Hush, my baby! if you don't,
  I shall find a way to treat you:
Hush, my baby! if you won't,
    Gaffer Grey shall come and eat you!
      Lullaby! do not cry!
      Gaffer Grey is coming by!

THE SONG OF THE NURSE.

Gaffer Grey has jaws, they say,
   Like a ramping roaring lion;
Masticating every day
   Whatsoe'er he casts his eye on.
      Lullaby! etc.

Greedily he swallows up
   All his friends can buy or borrow;
Bolts to-day a little cup,
   Gulps a long address to-morrow.
      Lullaby! etc.

Oh the dainties he has got
   In his terrible refectory!
Here a colonelcy, all hot,
   There a nicely roasted rectory.
      Lullaby! etc.

Though its perfume, he protests,
   Is of sulphur and of nitre,
He discusses and digests
   Now and then, a Bishop's mitre.
      Lullaby! etc.

Whensoe'er he wags his lip
   Just to chat, or just to chatter,

Down a score of trifles slip,
    No man caring for the matter.
        Lullaby! etc.

Clerkships, lordships, there they are;
    Half a hundred every quarter;
Now a ribbon, now a star,
    Here a cross, and there a garter.
        Lullaby! etc.

Pages at the palace say
    They have seen him—sad disaster!
Nibbling all the gems away
    From the sceptre of his master.
        Lullaby! etc.

When good people stop and stare,
    Saying to themselves, "Good gracious!
Did we e'er—oh no, we ne'er
    Saw a creature so voracious!"
        (Lullaby! etc.)

Mid the murmurs of the town,
    On the *Times* the monster gazes;
And, to wash his supper down,
    Swallows half a pipe of praises.
        Lullaby! etc.

THE SONG OF THE NURSE.

Hush, my baby! if you don't,
  I shall find a way to treat you:
Hush, my baby! if you won't,
  Gaffer Grey shall come and eat you!
    Lullaby! do not cry!
    Gaffer Grey is coming by!

XLV.

THE STATE OF THE NATION.

[In an article, well-reasoned but somewhat crudely expressed, which appeared in the *Times* of 10th March, 1834, there occurred the following passage :—" The tax on bread is a tyranny to which no human society ought to be subjected. Opinions may differ as to the rise or fall of prices after the repeal of this tax; if they do not fall, the landlords have nothing to deplore; if a fall has to be the consequence, we are now a trampled nation." This shot was fired in the *Morning Post*, the day after.—For Buckingham, now M.P. for Sheffield, see Part I. Nos. XX—XXII.—Mr. Gully, M.P. for Pontefract, had been a prizefighter in his youth, and made his money on the turf.—Mr. Pryme founded the Professorship of Political Economy at Cambridge, with the condition that he should himself be the first Professor.—Mr. Pease was M.P. for Durham Co.; for Fielden and Finn, see No. XXIX.]

"We are now a trampled nation."—*Times.*

WE have been some years reforming,
Chattering, cheering, stamping, storming;
Cutting bludgeons from the hedges,
Asking for all sorts of pledges;
Breaking heads, and breaking glasses,
Calling people knaves and asses;

After all our agitation,
We are now a " trampled nation " !

Mr. Croker's thrusts are parried,
Schedules A and B are carried ;
Vain is Wetherell's long alarum,
There is no reprieve for Sarum ;
All the money in our pockets
Went to purchase squibs and rockets;
Oh, what foolish exultation !
We are still " a trampled nation " !

Buckingham is quite a Tully,
Solon was a fool to Gully ;
Pryme's a lecturer, caught at college,
Pease, a Quaker, full of knowledge ;
Fielden is extremely clever,
Finn can talk, and talk for ever :
What a glorious constellation !
Yet we are " a trampled nation."

We have got Lord Grey to ease us
Of the taxes that displease us ;
We have got, besides, some dozens
Of his lordship's sons and cousins :

They are blest with places, pensions,
And the very best intentions;
It's against their inclination
That we are "a trampled nation."

We have got the *Times* adorning
Facts with figures every morning;
Now denouncing right and reason,
Now defending guilt and treason;
Raving, ranting, blustering, blundering,
Pro and con alternate thundering;
It has wondrous circulation;
Why are we "a trampled nation"?

XLVI.

A MEMBER'S MUSINGS.

[14th March, 1834.]

" Lord Althorp made a reply, but, as is almost invariably the case, the noble lord was perfectly inaudible in the gallery."
" The reply of the noble lord was again perfectly inaudible to any one in the gallery "—*House of Commons Report, Tuesday, March 11th.*

" ORDER, order ! "—" Bar, bar ! "—" Door, door ! "
Such are the cries as he stands on the floor,
Waving his hand for a little while,
And wreathing his lip in a gentle smile :
We stoop our head, we strain our ear ;
Nobody hears him ;—" Hear, hear, hear ! "

What is he talking of ?—figures or facts ?
Liberal principles ?—Algerine acts ?
The rise of the unions, or of stocks ?
The weight of the debt, or the last prize ox ?

Crops or cholera?—Jews or beer?
All of them!—none of them!—" Hear, hear, hear!"

Quick is O'Connell in debate;
Cunning is Hume to calculate;
But Hume and O'Connell their way will miss,
Trying to answer a speech like this!
" When it's a proper time to cheer,
Wake me, dear Ellice!"—" Hear, hear, hear!"

There is a lady in a play,
Who speaks, though she does nothing say;
Fortune has brought us a lord in her freaks,
Who just says nothing, though he speaks.
What in the papers will appear?
Only " Lord Althorp," and " Hear, hear, hear!"

XLVII.

COUNSELS OF A FATHER TO HIS SON.

[15th March, 1834. Lord Plunket was one of the Ecclesiastical Commissioners for Ireland, who reported, in 1831, in favour of the separation of the six parishes comprised in the Deanery of Down. He appointed his son, the Honourable and Reverend Robert Plunket, to the vacant Deanery the year after. His nepotism had been the subject of a witty and violent attack by Cobbett, in the *Political Register*, in which an early speech of his, devoting his children, like Hamilcar, to the contest with England over Catholic Emancipation, was very effectively employed against him. On the 11th March Mr. Goulburn called attention to this appointment; the defence made for Lord Plunket will be found in the debates of the 16th.]

"Down, Derry Down!'—*Old Song*.

When I at last shall sleep in peace,
When life's consumption shall be o'er,
When I shall fill that payless place
Where none shall plot or plunder more
Remember on what wings I soared
To infamy's unfading crown,
How I became a noble lord,
And you became the Dean of Down.

Professing disregard of self,
    I won the ermine of a Peer;
Avowing carelessness of pelf,
    I earned some thousand pounds a year;
I caught the favours of the Court,
    And seemed as honest as a clown;
And though I fathered a "Report,"
    I fathered, too, the Dean of Down.

By turns with every party leagued,
    As each by turns might rise or fall,
I blustered, bullied, schemed, intrigued,
    Was loved by none, was used by all;
Placeman and patriot, both for pay,
    I flinched not from the general frown—
I am the Chancellor to-day,
    And you to-day the Dean of Down.

If I on this world's busy stage
    Had worshipped honour, followed truth,
Less praise would gild my hoary age,
    Less hope would greet your sanguine youth.
If blameless I my gown had worn,
    I still might wear my plain stuff gown;
If I had shrunk from public scorn,
    You would not be the Dean of Down.

Go forth and do as I have done,
    Like glory on your pathway shine;
Mine be your principles, my son,
    And be your profits more than mine;
Haste, worthy of your sire's embrace,
    To emulate your sire's renown;
Be false and factious, bold and base,
    And make your son the Dean of Down!

XLVIII.

THE WHISPERS OF THE RUE RIVOLI.

[12th May, 1834.—Some of the prominent Ministerialists had visited Paris during the Whitsun vacation. Lord Durham was now anxious to return to power, and Mr. Ellice to be in the Cabinet.— "A person discreditably known in the city"—"who ought long ago to have shrunk into privacy" was actual language employed by the *Times* of the latter, in relation to his concern, with Hume and Bowring, in the affair of the Greek loan (See Part I., No. VI.)].

"He points to Lord Durham in the *salons*, and whispers, 'That is the man!'"—*Morning Post.*

Who will come to the place some day—
The pleasant place, where dear Lord Grey
Just now so tenderly feeds some dozens
Of patriot sons and patriot cousins?
Who from the national purse will draw
All that is left by his father-in-law?
Who will end what Grey began?
That is the man! That is the man!

Who in due time will make of me,
Though in the city I may be

"Very discreditably known,"
Because of my share in a certain loan,
Who in due time will make me yet
A member of the Cabinet,
Ruling with him his dark divan?
That is the man! That is the man!

Who, though I ought with Hume and Co.
To have shrunk into privacy long ago,
Will bring me the book, over whose long leaves
Honest Lord Althorp growls and grieves,
The ledger of the bankrupt state,
That I may carefully calculate
And glean from the ruin all I can?
That is the man! That is the man!

Who will saunter to Court, and sing
A pretty song to our Lord the King,
Of peers in treason foul arrayed,
Of wicked plots by bishops laid,
Of loyalty spouting from Radical Clubs,
Of piety driven to preach from tubs?
Who will Royalty's wits trepan?
That is the man! That is the man!

Who by and by, when a maiden Queen
Shall on our tottering throne be seen,

All too weak to stem the storm
Which we philosophers call " Reform "—
Who will condescend to hold
Robe of state and sceptre of gold,
Leaving her Majesty frock and fan ?
That is the man ! That is the man !

Who will abolish the mitre and crown,
And pull the Church and the Palace down ?
Who will burn, at the public charge,
The Bible and Prayer-book and statutes at large ?
Who will annul and annihilate quite
All the old maxims of wrong and right,
And govern the world on a nice new plan ?
That is the man ! That is the man !

XLIX.

THE FALSE REPORT.

[17th May, 1834.—The resignations of Mr. Stanley and Sir James Graham were now impending. "The wish was father to the thought," when the *Morning Post* announced that Lord Palmerston also was believed to be meditating resignation.—The "old man" is, of course, Talleyrand, still Minister in England for the French Government.]

"We must condole with the *Post*. Lord Palmerston has not resigned.'
Globe, May 16th, 1834.

THERE's no foundation for the news,
 Whate'er the sanguine *Post* may say;
England has commerce yet to lose,
 And friendships yet to cast away.
Dead are her laurels, dim her fame;
 But destiny has yet behind
A darker doom, a fouler shame;
 Lord Palmerston has not resigned!

What happy tidings these must be
 For all who hate our name and race!

King Leopold is full of glee,
    Don Pedro wears a cheerful face;
And yon old man with ringlets white,
    The lame, who loves to lead the blind,
Is merry o'er his cards to-night;
    Lord Palmerston has not resigned!

The scornful look, the angry tone,
    Are vain in our degenerate days;
Resigned? Oh no! high hearts alone
    Can rightly value blame or praise.
A nation's sneer, a nation's frown,
    Might awe, might fire, a noble mind;
Pitt would have flung his office down!—
    Lord Palmerston has not resigned.

L.

A FAMILIAR EPISTLE.

FROM DUDLEY TO EDINBURGH.

[20th May, 1834.—See No. XLI. This piece does not appear in the edition privately printed. As Attorney General, Sir John Campbell had prosecuted the *True Sun* for a seditious libel, in advocating the non-payment of taxes, pending the adoption by the ministry of the advanced Radical programme. Counsel for defendants quoted Lord Milton's famous sentiment, and Mr. W. Brougham's advice to the tax-gatherer to "call again." Campbell had nothing to plead but that these were hasty utterances, not reduced to writing by their authors. He obtained a conviction.]

"Look, here comes a lover of mine, and a lover of hers."—*As You Like It.*

Sir John is a terrible man,
   He is born pretty towns to beguile;
Beware—oh beware—if you can,
   Of the magic that lurks in his smile:
Though soft his entreaties may be,
   I've heard him as tenderly sue:
For he used to come courting to me,
   As now he goes courting to you.

A tricolor banner he bore
  To render his principles plain;
A tricolor ribbon he wore;
  He'll probably wear it again.
With his conduct, I quickly could see,
  His colours had little to do;
But oh! they were lovely to me,
  And oh! they'll be lovely to you.

He taught me, the villain, to hope,
  Such blessings as eye never saw;
Cheap raiment, cheap victuals, cheap soap,
  Cheap learning, cheap churches, cheap law.
You'd have thought that he spoke for a fee,
  So moving his eloquence grew;
The arts that could fascinate me—
  Oh will they not fascinate you?

He promised the people his aid,
  He gave it to Althorp and Grey;
A Radical here while he stayed,
  A Whig when he trotted away.
He swore that the Press should be free,
  And straight an indictment he drew;
A sad disappointment to me,
  A sad disappointment to you!

But take him; a seat must be had
    For Mr. Attorney, no doubt:
Do take him; Lord Althorp is sad
    While his learned adviser is out.
Since " off with the old love " is he,
    It's time to be " on with the new;"
Detected, rejected by me,
    Pray take him—I leave him to you!

LI.

COLLOQUIES OF THE CANONGATE.

[23d May, 1834.—The same subject is pursued. This also was omitted in the printed edition.—For the *True Sun*, see the notes on the last piece.—Sir Charles Pepys, the Solicitor-General, was an infrequent and unready speaker, and Campbell, in his Autobiography, ascribes an important defeat of the Government, in the case of Baron Smith, an Irish judge, considered by them to have made a political charge from the Bench, to their lack of legal assistance, due to his own temporary exclusion from the House.]

"Rem populi tractas."—Pers.

Whence do you come, Sir knight, Sir knight,
So gloomy and glum, Sir knight, Sir knight?
 "From Dudley, where stories
 Invented by Tories
Have ruined my character quite, quite,
Have ruined my character quite."

Who bade you appear, Sir knight, Sir knight,
To dazzle us here, Sir knight, Sir knight?

"Lord Althorp, in trouble
That Pepys, my double,
Is not very ready to fight, fight,
Is not very ready to fight."

What have you got, Sir knight, Sir knight.
To bother the Scot, Sir knight, Sir knight?
   "A bow and a bag
   And a tricolor flag
And speeches well sprinkled with spite, spite,
And speeches well sprinkled with spite."

What have you done, Sir knight, Sir knight,
About the *True Sun*, Sir knight, Sir knight?
   "I've shown that with reason
   A Lord may talk treason
Which a Commoner ought not to write, write,
Which a Commoner ought not to write."

What shall we see, Sir knight, Sir knight,
If we make you M.P., Sir knight, Sir knight?
   "You'll see me depart
   With my hand on my heart,
Very grateful and very polite,—lite,
Very grateful and very polite."

How will you cure, Sir knight, Sir knight,
The ills we endure, Sir knight, Sir knight?
 "I've just got a notion
 Of making a motion
That black shall in future be white, white,
That black shall in future be white."

LII.

THE LATE RESIGNATIONS.

[June 25th, 1834.—The session had been largely occupied with an Irish Church Bill, to which Stanley had given his consent with difficulty. By this were renewed the clauses which had been struck out by the House of Lords from the Bill of the year before. When on a motion of Mr. Ward, M.P., the Ministers responsible for the Bill showed a willingness to make yet further concessions, Mr. Stanley and Sir James Graham (May 27th) resigned office, and were followed by the Duke of Richmond, and by the Earl of Ripon (formerly Lord Goderich). A series of articles in the *Morning Post*, of Praed's writing, had foretold the catastrophe, and urged resignation upon the wavering statesmen.—Sir Samuel Whalley, the proprietor of a private asylum, was M.P. for Marylebone.—Mr. Ellice by these resignations obtained a seat in the Cabinet. Lord Durham was, however, excluded; by Lord Brougham's jealousy, as some thought; but the dislike of him was widespread among his old colleagues.]

"Vivant Arturius illic
Et Catulus."—JUV.

'TWAS time for this; too long, too long,
In sad communion of disgrace,
The right have banded with the wrong,
The pure have herded with the base,

Sense should not be to Quackery tied,
  Nor Piety be linked with Cant,
Nor Graham sit by Thomson's side,
  Nor Stanley share the shame of Grant.

'Twas time for this; they are not fit
  To flatter Finn, conciliate Grote,
To shake their sides at Whalley's wit
  And strain their voice for Gully's vote;
To covet Burdett's ready smiles,
  To credit oaths by Harvey sworn,
And soothe with diplomatic wiles
  The burly beggar's hate and scorn.

'Twas time for this; when general gloom
  Enwraps whate'er we deem divine,
When madness speaks the common doom
  Of crown and mitre, throne and shrine,
'Twas time to leave you shameful seat
  To men of fitting heart and head;
The drum should be by Ellice beat;
  The march should be by Durham led!

[Note.—The above was the last of these pieces acknowledged by Praed. Although I think I can trace Praed's writing, in the *Morning Post*, at intervals, up to the final dismissal of the Whig Ministry, under Lord Melbourne's Premiership, on the 17th November, yet after August 1834 it is no longer as a regular writer that he figures in its columns, and none of the poetry appears to me to be from his pen. The following are probably by E. M. Fitzgerald; 11th July, 1834, *The Way to Win him*, 15th July, *Translation of a recent Speech*; 22nd July, *The Juvenile Whig*; 30th July, *Ode to Lord Mulgrave*; 5th August, *Speech on the Poor Laws Amendment Bill*; 9th April, 1835, *Epithalamium for April the 11th*; 20th April, *Musings by the Serpentine*; 15th September, *Lines to a New Pensioner*. If on a comparison of these undoubtedly clever imitations with the poems acknowledged by Praed, it should appear to any future critic that they have been rejected, as his, on too slight grounds, I can only ask that some regard may be paid to the opinion of those who have carefully examined them all, with the aid of letters, recollections, and scrap books of the period, and have decided on the balance of many small considerations, which it would be wearisome in every case to enumerate. The constant use of italics, the absurd misprints, due probably to his bad handwriting, and the blunders in Latin, are marks of Fitzgerald that can hardly be mistaken; and I think, in spite of his attempts to copy closely the ease of Praed's manner, there are hardly ever a dozen consecutive lines of his, in which the inferiority of workmanship does not somehow show itself.]

LIII.

THE SONG OF THE BELLS.

[This piece exists only in MS. so far as I know, and without date. Lord Grey was so often reported to be on the point of resignation, that it is difficult to say exactly to which occasion it is to be referred. He finally resigned, as a result of the Brougham-Wellesley-Littleton intrigue with O'Connell, on July 9th, 1834. But the true date of this poem was no doubt earlier; for Waithman died in 1833, and Sir T. Denman was raised to the Bench in November of the same year.]

"Turn again, Whittington.'

Oh, whither does your Lordship run
    In such a fume and fret?
Your task is only just begun,
    We cannot spare you yet:
You know there's nothing half so sweet
    As power, and place, and pay;
You can't be tired of Downing Street;
    Oh, turn again, Lord Grey.

And you will have your Peers, no doubt,
    To serve you, thick and thin;

THE SONG OF THE BELLS.

To wait upon your going out
    And on your coming in;
And fools and flatterers, slaves and thieves,
    Will play a pretty play
With little balls and strawberry leaves;
    So turn again, Lord Grey.

And you'll be lauded in the *Globe*,
    And laurelled in the *Times*;
And painted in a Roman robe,
    And sung in scurvy rhymes:
The spouting-clubs will play their pranks
    To make their master gay;
They'll smother you with votes of thanks—
    Quick, turn again, Lord Grey.

And Hume and Harvey will declare
    You speak their very tone;
And Duncombe will devoutly swear
    Your heart is like his own:
For you will noisy Denman bawl
    And empty Waithman bray;
And you will learn to love them all—
    There, turn again, Lord Grey.

LIV.

LINES.

WRITTEN UNDER A PORTRAIT OF LORD MAYO, DRAWN
BY THE QUEEN.

[This little piece was written in an Album of Lady Mayo's which contained more than one of Queen Adelaide's sketches. See Praed's Collected Poems, Vol. I., pp. 367—371. Lady Mayo was Praed's aunt.]

A COURTIER of the nobler sort,
 A Christian of the purer school,
Tory, when Whigs are great at Court,
 And Protestant, when Papists rule—

Prompt to support the monarch's crown,
 As prompt to dry the poor man's tears,
Yet fearing not the rabble's frown,
 And seeking not the rabble's cheers—

Still ready—favoured or disgraced—
 To do the right, to speak the true —
The Artist who these features traced
 A better Subject never knew!

POLITICAL AND OCCASIONAL POEMS.

PART III.

1839.

Ⅰ.

THE CONTESTED ELECTION.

TO VISCOUNT MORPETH, M.P.

[These three satires, the second in an unfinished state, were found among the poet's MSS. after his death. They were written in the winter of 1838-9, at a time when his health had begun to fail, but before any cause for serious anxiety had revealed itself. The declining prestige of the Whig Government, the unsatisfactory state of the law as to corruption and intimidation at elections, and the personal characteristics of Lord Palmerston and Lord Melbourne as public men, are the subjects which come uppermost. The session of 1838 had been in many respects an unsatisfactory one. The authority of the Speaker had been challenged, several "rows" had occurred, and not much business had been done.

This piece must have been written when the author was away from his books of reference, for he wrote it under the impression that Lord Morpeth was now "member for the independent Borough of Malton," whereas he was member for the West Riding. Malton was represented by Lord Milton and Mr. Childers.—For a collection of the declarations of "finality" made by eminent Liberals after the passing of the Reform Bill, see Praed's article in the *Morning Post* of January 29th, 1833.—For Doctor Carpue, see Part II., No. XIII.—After the resignation of Stanley, Graham and the rest, in May 1834, an address was got up by Lord Ebrington, and presented to Lord Grey by members of his party, expressive of their continued confidence in his administration. In his reply the Premier took occasion to deprecate "the constant and active pressure from without," which, he said, was urging the Ministry to the adoption of measures, the necessity of which was not fully proved. This referred especially to Mr. Ward's motion for a committee, with a view to "reduce the Irish Church Establishment," by "vital and extensive changes."—Messrs. Shaw and Lefroy were members for Dublin University; Mr. Ward for Sheffield, Mr. Grote for the City of London, and Messrs. Wakley and Duncombe for Finsbury. —Sir Hussey Vivian sat for East Cornwall; he voted for the Ballot on the 15th February, 1838; he had walked out, rather than vote, the previous year.—Mr. Warburton, on 6th December, 1837, had said, in a sensible speech on Mr. Blewitt's motion (see No. III.),—"All knew that as money constituted the sinews of war, so it was the means by which petitions were persevered in.' —Mr. Smith, M.P. for High Wycombe, after an expensive career, had just succeeded his father as Lord Carrington. Mr. Nurse was unsuccessful in his candidature.—The famous "horse-pond" article in the *Times* of April 30th, has already been referred to, Part II., No. IV. It was an elaborate picture of the treatment reserved for Anti-Reform candidates.—"We see him, in our mind's eye, present himself to the people; we hear the groans which at first assail him; we see the first discharge of mud, dead cats, and rotten eggs, which encircle his bare and devoted head. Then, as the populace becomes more determined, and more excited, we see the pebbles and gravel begin to fly; these are succeeded by paving-stones, bricks, etc.; and the Corinthian capital of Toryism is forced to retire with a broken head! . . . Now, do we approve of such scenes as these? Quite the contrary, we deprecate them beforehand, and shall deplore them if they take place. But, etc., . . . once again, we warn them to desist; . . . in every borough-town will they meet the reception we have just pictured: they will become acquainted with every village pump; the clear river and the muddy pool will alike receive them; they will carry away undesired samples of the soil of each county, and will consider themselves fortunate if contumely and contusions be all they meet with."—Mr. John E. Elliott, son to the Earl of Minto, was M.P. for Roxburghshire. A debate was raised May 24th, 1838, as to rioting which had occurred at Hawick at the election; the sitting member declared there had been "no riots which could be so called;" "misconduct and violence he did not deny." Somebody indeed had been thrown into the river; but it was only two feet deep; "about sax or twal inches," according to one witness. Somebody, certainly, had been wounded with an "unlawful weapon"; but it was, in fact, "with a pin."—Mr. Coppock was the manager of elections for the central Liberal Association. His name was unpleasantly prominent when, at a later date, St. Albans and Sudbury were disfranchised for corrupt practices.—Mr. M. D. Hill had a parliamentary practice; he had been M.P. for Hull.—Sir George Strickland was Lord Morpeth's colleague in the representation of the West Riding.—Praed had spoken well in a debate of 2nd April, 1838, seriously impugning the system under which Committees of the House of Commons, consisting of party men, attempted to exercise judicial functions in matters of controverted functions; and he gave a pledge of sincerity on that occasion, by voting with O'Connell, against both Peel and Russell, for inquiry, with a view to reform.]

'TIS sweet, when winds are lashing ocean
Into a terrible commotion,
Amidst the elemental roar
To fold one's arms upon the shore,
And see another, friend or stranger,
Tossed to and fro in mortal danger.
'Tis sweet, when on a field of battle
The sabres flash, the bullets rattle,
To choose an elevated spot,
Beyond the reach of shell or shot,
And watch the heroes taking pains
To batter out each other's brains.
In language somewhat more sublime
  So said a fine old Roman poet;
But had he lived to know our time
  As you, my lord, already know it,

Another verse he might have wrought,
  Not less sonorous, to assure us
That of all sweets 'tis sweetest thought
  By all the herd of Epicurus,
When writs are flying up and down,
And folk, in country and in town,
With drums and trumpets, feasts and fights,
Are making burgesses and knights,
To drive from Malton, quite delighted
At finding Malton so united,
And mark how people rob and gull
Some luckless friend at York or Hull.

Hard, very hard, the patriot's fate,
  Whom Brooks's and the stars send down
To be the Liberal candidate
  For some extremely liberal town!
Who quits his house in sweet May Fair
  In vain regretting and repining,
While Fashion in her glory there
  Is fiddling, flirting, dancing, dining—
Who drops the visit that was planned
  To Naples by his wife and daughters,
Or that which Clarke and Keate command
  To Cheltenham for a course of waters—
Who rattles from his country seat
  When hounds are meeting all about him,

Or steals away from Lombard Street
  When business can't go on without him—
Who leaves, in short, by hurried stages
  Whate'er amuses or engages,
And, hanging out a ponderous flag
On Crown or Castle, Star or Stag,
By speech and placard makes it clear
To all who see, and all who hear,
That he's the man to represent
The march of mind in Parliament,
And play the champion or the martyr,
Next session, for the People's Charter.

Hark, 'tis a fine barouche and four!
  The ostlers to the gate are springing;
Bright eyes peep out at every door;
  From every tower the bells are ringing.
Awakened to his country's call,
  His broadsides say to all who read 'em,
Sir Felix Froth, of Frothy Hall,
  Invites us, one and all, to freedom!

Sir Felix Froth we must admit
A moderate Whig, of moderate wit;
He sips his wine, he taps his box,
And lauds the memory of Fox;
He thinks all jobs extremely dirty,
But has not heard of one since 'thirty;

He hailed Reform with pride and pleasure,
But calls the Act a " final measure."
Like great Earl Grey, whose nerves were shocked
One day when Doctor Carpue knocked,
Sir Felix looks with dread and doubt
Upon the " pressure from without ;"
Like small Lord John, who now grows sick
Of argument by stone and stick,
Sir Felix cries, " The Constitution
Don't want an annual Revolution."
If Knatchbull's doctrine seems to him
A superannuated whim,
It does not follow he should vote
With Mr. Ward or Mr. Grote ;
And if he'd lend his help with joy
To stifle Shaw or gag Lefroy,
That can't imply an approbation
Of all O'Connell's agitation.
In short, Sir Felix would suggest
That movement's safest when at rest,
And hint that Freedom would be better
For here a bolt, and there a fetter.
Alas! Sir Felix will discover,
Ere half his canvass shall be over,
That sound opinions on demand
Advance, recede, contract, expand ;
That choice of right and wrong depends
Upon the wishes of one's friends ;

That all from time must wisdom borrow;
That white to-day is black to-morrow;
And that it's hard, in public station,
Midst all the changes of creation,
While winds and waters veer and vary,
Super antiquas vias stare.

Old Shears the tailor, who has long
    Been sagest of the clubroom sages,
Learned in Paine, in Cobbett strong,
    And deep in Bentham's lucid pages—
In whose mysterious shop are wrought,
    Not vests alone, but systems, newer
Than any that have yet been taught
    By any Westminster Reviewer—
Protests that Whig and Tory both
Are cut from just the selfsame cloth;
Avows that from his very heart he
Abhors the name of either party;
And, when his man begins to wheedle,
Is quite intent upon his needle.
Harmodius Nibbs, the fierce conductor
Of every poor man's " best instructor,"
Who by an inch of odorous taper
Compiles the Independent Paper,
And racks his brain and dims his eyes
In calling names and coining lies,

Through two laborious columns simmers
Against all waverers and trimmers;
Applauds his own impartial pen,
And roars for "measures," not for "men."
And soon the Union frankly states
By half a dozen delegates—
Undaunted patriots, who assemble
   In council at the Cato's Head,
To make confederate tyrants tremble
   And deprecate the tax on bread—
That they've prepared a little string
Of questions about everything,
To which they're anxious he should say
His "yes," or "no," without delay;
And, since they all desire to show
   How very deeply they respect him,
They'll pelt him if he answers "no,"
   And if he answers "yes," elect him.

Sir Felix fancies that he sees
Clearer and clearer by degrees.
Six years ago, he hoped and trusted,
The franchise had been well adjusted;
But yet the virtue of the invention
May be improved by some extension;
He's quite convinced—he may be wrong—
That Parliaments don't last too long;

But their duration, on reflection,
May be curtailed without objection;
He feels that every honest man
Will poll in public, if he can,
But votes for ballot, when he's bid,
As meekly as Sir Hussey did.

These trifles settled—presto, pass!
   The Baronet becomes a hero,
And sees his hopes in fortune's glass
   Mount up to summer heat from zero.
And now he valorously fights
The battle of the many's rights;
Surfeits at taverns, smokes at clubs,
Harangues from wagons and from tubs;
Delights all hearers and beholders,
And rides on independent shoulders.
Whene'er he speaks, the gazers own
He speaks with Wakley's silver tone;
Whene'er he stops, the gazers vow
He stops with Duncombe's graceful bow.
The ladies take prodigious pride
In broidering banners six yards wide;
The schoolboys, hurrying from their broth,
Shout "Froth for ever, vote for Froth!"

War's sinews are of gold, they say;
   Since never yet from empty pockets

Came spear and shield in Cæsar's day,
  In Wellington's, grenades and rockets:
And soon Sir Felix is afraid,
  In spite of chairing and of cheering,
That not of cheaper stuff are made
  The sinews of electioneering.

"Another thousand!—bless my heart!
Upon my life you make me start;
You can't persuade me, in my senses,
It's all 'legitimate expenses.'
When Parliament with such applause
Destroyed St. Michael's and St. Mawes—
Excuse me, Sir—I really thought,
That seats were never to be bought;
That candidates were not to hear
Of flagmen, stavesmen, breakfasts, beer;
In short, that we had full security
For perfect principle and purity."
Fine phrases! but it seems the game
Continues pretty much the same;
And Liberal sentiments don't weigh,
Unless combined with liberal pay.
"For Queen and Country one is willing,
Of course, to lavish every shilling;
But, Sir, one's family, 'tis true,
Must sometimes be remembered too.

Miss Froth—my Lady hints, with reason—
May want a settlement next season;
And Harry will be begging soon
Papa to make him a dragoon.
I don't complain—the honour's such—
But, hang it! it might cost too much."

When first from hand of truant Will
A stone goes rolling down a hill,
So slow it starts, with every hop
You think it's coming to a stop.
If in the middle of its journey
You touch it, it may chance to burn ye:
And do but look how very fast
It leaps to level ground at last.
Thus wise Sir Felix, first intending
The greatest caution in descending,
Quickens his pace as he advances,
Discards his conscientious fancies,
Sends tickets out as thick as hail,
Floods all the market place with ale,
Sells out his tranquil Three per Cents,
Anticipates his Christmas rents,
And thinks as lightly of his purse
As Mr. Smith or Mr. Nurse.

Yet after all the cost and pain
   Bestowed on dinners and on speeches,

Some few are found, whose stubborn brain
   Nor rhetoric nor rhino reaches :
Some few incorrigible Tories,
   Who fancy all they read is true
Of Britain's liberties and glories,
   Of Trafalgar and Waterloo ;
Who say a nation ought to be
Contented to be great and free,
And call it sin to seek aught further
By arson, robbery and murder ;
Who hold the country of their birth
The finest country upon earth,
And will not for instruction go
To Jefferson or Mirabeau ;
Odd men, and willing to be odd,
Who read their Bible, serve their God,
And snap their fingers at the Pope,
And wish O'Connell in a rope.
On such dull bigots soft coercion
May work, perhaps, a late conversion.
When logic fails in grave debate,
A brickbat often carries weight ;
When prejudice is proof 'gainst wit,
A club may make a happier hit ;
Where these no good effect produce,
A horse pond will be found of use.
Sir Felix, most humane of men,
   Looks vastly serious now and then ;

Assures the Mayor he hates a riot,
And begs reformers to be quiet;
But yet his stiff respect for law
In proper time begins to thaw;
He vows it's monstrously ill-bred
　To take a friendly joke in dudgeon;
He half suspects that Tory head
　Was only made for Liberal bludgeon;
He sees, as plain as noonday sun
　That might is right, when Whigs employ it;
And finally, enjoys the fun
　As Johnny Elliot might enjoy it.

A minute more—another second—
The poll is closed; the votes are reckoned.
What if Sir Felix finds his place
Is just the hindmost in the race?
Repulsed to-day, he yet may rally
His forces for to-morrow's sally.
Soon, to redeem his lost position,
Coppock shall frame him a petition;
A Whig Committee, nothing loath,
Shall at the table take the oath;
Hired witnesses with tales shall ply 'em
For only two pounds two *per diem;*
While Hill shall jumble law and fact,
Misstate the case, misquote the Act;

And lest some unit of the quorum
Should have a fancy for decorum,
And stumble on the least pretence
To Common Law, or common sense,
The Fates shall take peculiar care
To put a Strickland in the chair.

II.

THE POLITICAL DRAWING-ROOM.

TO LADY———.

[It is impossible to assign any individuality at this distance of time, either to the fair lady honoured with this dedication, or to the "Lady Daisy" who is satirized. Probably no particular allusion was intended, for it was Praed's rule to abstain from bringing ladies into party politics.—There were at this time two Zoological Gardens in London; that in Surrey was afterwards given up.—Sir Matthew Wood in 1838 carried the Hackney Carriages Regulation Bill; but the second reading of it was once counted out, on February 28th.—The Christinos, the supporters of Regent Queen Christina in Spain, were the constitutional, the Carlists, the legitimist party.—John Wood was an authority on educational matters, an Edinburgh Benthamite; John Stuart Mill requires no note; Joseph Hume was now M.P. for Kilkenny, by he grace of O'Connell; Joseph Parkes was a Birmingham solicitor, author of the *History of the Court of Chancery*, and brains-carrier to Mr. Attwood's Political Union.—Sir John Campbell, the Attorney-General, in 1836 secured a peerage for his wife, and in 1841 another for himself. His quarrel was rather with the law lords than with the Peerage: he was counsel for the House of Commons in the ridiculous case of Stockdale *v.* Hansard.—Colonel Perronet Thompson was a great champion of Free Trade, a voluminous writer, and a very trenchant speaker

Compare Sir Alexander Boswell's reply to Dr. Johnson, who asked him, "What good did Cromwell ever do?"—"Doctor, he gart kings ken that they had a lith in their necks." This allusion to the day when Republican-minded under graduates used to dine on "Calf's head," seems to show that the accusation rather spitefully brought against the author by Bulwer Lytton and Professor Pryme, on 27th June, 1838, of having been present on such an occasion, in his salad days, at Cambridge, had not permanently afflicted him; though it caused him some loss of his temper at the time.—Charles Buller, M.P. for Liskeard, Thomas Carlyle's pupil, and a rising Whig politician, was often pitted by his friends against Praed, whom he resembled in the too early termination of his career. See Bulwer Lytton's *St. Stephen's* for a genial estimate of both, written long after.]

FAIR Lady, nor less good than fair,
 When I have watched your various bounty
Diffusing, like the liberal air,
 Its love and life through half the county;
When I have seen, in hut or shed,
 By which your fairy foot has glided,
The supper dressed, the pillow spread,
 The fuel stored, the drug provided;
When I have witnessed round your path
Averted vengeance, softened wrath—
The sluggard roused to honest labour,
The miser won to clothe his neighbour,
The tears of sorrow wiped away,
The lips of childhood taught to pray;
Thus, I have thought, to clasp the tie
That links the humble to the high,

To make the coronet more bright
Before a grateful people's sight,
And show in wealth the copious source
Whence mercy takes its constant course—
This, more than sharp and shrill debate
About the sins of Church or State,
Is noble Woman's public duty—
The patriotism of British beauty.

But belles there are, whose proud enjoyment
Affects a more sublime enjoyment;
Who love their country with such kindness,
Despite its baseness and its blindness,
That, not content to charm and bless it,
They must reform it and redress it;
Who, bright with every natural grace,
With ——'s figure, ——'s face,
To make themselves quite overpowering,
Must write like Bentham, talk like Bowring.

Go, gaze on all the wondrous things,
   The skinny, scaly, feathery, furry,
Which science from the wide world brings
   To pine in Middlesex and Surrey—
Read tomes of travels—Clarke's and Cook's—
   And lounge through gallery and Museum,
And open all the folio books
   Of pictures at the Athenæum;

You'll own at last, of all the creatures,
    With various forms and various features,
That daily walk, and swim, and fly
    About the earth, the sea, the sky,
You find the oddest on your notes—
    A Radical in petticoats.

Thanks to Sir Matthew's useful Bill,
    Once more the house is counted out;
We'll step to George Street if you will,
    And look at Lady Daisy's Rout.

Since every beast and every bird
    In the huge Ark together trembled,
Oh when was such a motley herd
    Of living creatures e'er assembled?
Quacks, knaves of every rank and station
And creed and tongue and hue and nation,
Precursors, Liberators, Chartists,
Christinos, Masons, Bonapartists,
Cigar consumers, opium chewers,
Bad novelists and worse reviewers,
Commissioners, inspectors, clerks,
John Wood, John Mill, Joe Hume, Joe Parkes!
Sweet Lady Daisy, formed by Venus
Best specimen of all the genus—
For since man's ears by trash were tickled
Trash ne'er from lips more lovely trickled—

Oh what could make her, with those eyes
　As deeply blue as summer's heaven,
So sagely witty, gaily wise,
　And hardly—hardly twenty-seven,
With such a person, such a purse,
　So many thousand pounds and graces,
With such a pen for prose and verse,
　Such taste in lovers and in laces—
Oh what could make her bear to be
The very curious thing we see?
A radiant jewel vilely set,
Half Jacobin and half coquette,
A rebel in the softest silks,
A kind of muslin Mr. Wilkes,
Bright student, but of dullest knowledge,
Fair scholar, but in foulest college,
In spite of nature's lavished store—
Youth, beauty, talent, wit—a bore!
When Johnny Campbell, in a queer rage,
Denounces all the British Peerage,
And tears to rags the robe his heir
A few years hence intends to wear—
When Joseph Hume, the cunning man,
　The wondrous Cocker of Kilkenny,
Elucidates the newest plan
　To spend a pound and spare a penny—
When Colonel Thompson's loyal warning
Reminds us of the hallowed morning

On which prophetic cricks perplex
The stiffness of all royal necks—
When Lord John Russell vents his spleen
Against a Bishop or a Dean—
When great O'Connell dubs at once
Wellesley a dastard, Peel a dunce,
The world admits, in all such cases,
How well the work the workman graces;
But out alas!—'tis what in France
   Our neighbours call a "false position,"
When elephants will hornpipes dance,
   Or Lady Daisy lisp sedition!

What strange and unconnected matter
You hear the lovely lady chatter!
'Tis now the Spirit of the Time,
   And now the fashions of the season,
And here a little bit of rhyme,
   And there a little bit of reason;
That clever paper in the *Globe*,
And Lady Jersey's charming robe;
Ingenious Carson's newest toque,
And funny Buller's latest joke;
Deep thoughts upon the nation's debt,
Fine praise of Elsler's pirouette,
[Sermons] against patrician vices,
And eulogies of Gunter's ices!
   *   *   *   *

III.
THE TREASURY BENCH.

TO VISCOUNT PALMERSTON.

[LORD PALMERSTON first entered Parliament in 1806, and took office in 1807. He was then continuously in office until 1828; and after a short stay in opposition under Wellington, was Foreign Minister in all the Liberal administrations between 1830 and 1851, Home Secretary in Lord Aberdeen's administration, 1852-1855, and then Prime Minister, with a short interlude in 1858-9, till his death in 1865; total, forty-nine years of office in fifty-nine of public life.—For Colonel Evans, see Pt. II., No. XXX.; Mr. Leader was now his colleague in the representation of Westminster.— The Marquis of Normanby, till recently Lord Mulgrave, was Lord Lieutenant of Ireland; he had written three novels, *Contrast, Matilda,* and *Yes and No.*—Lord Melbourne was credited with a common form of reply to troublesome colleagues, who wanted to pass measures—"Can't you let it alone?"—Mr. E. J. Stanley, afterwards Lord Stanley of Alderley, was M.P. for North Cheshire, and Treasury Whip.—Lord Durham was sent to Canada on a mission which resulted, on the whole, in restoring order and satisfaction with the Government, though some illegal acts were committed, which injured his reputation for ability. —Sugden and Follett had been Sir R. Peel's Attorney and Solicitor-General in 1835.—Mr. Blewitt on the 6th December, 1837, in a pompous speech, moved a series of resolutions, directed against a fund, of which Mr. Andrew Spottiswoode was treasurer, which had been subscribed for the purpose of prosecuting petitions against the elections of O'Connellites. After a slashing answer from Lord Stanley, he tried to withdraw his motion, and a scene of tremendous confusion ensued. The next night things were still worse. The Speaker led off, with a rather maudlin protest against the way the House had treated him the night before; and then Smith O'Brien moved, and Bulwer Lytton seconded, a similar resolution to Mr. Blewitt's. The debate is memorable for the exhibitions made of themselves by three great exhibitors; Sir Francis Burdett, for the last time of many; O'Connell, in perhaps his most conspicuous performance of the kind; and Disraeli, in his celebrated maiden speech. Nothing came of it all.—Lord Plunket in one of his famous speeches on the Catholic claims, delivered in 1824, after describing how Governments should watch and direct the changes of public sentiment, said—" If this were not the spirit which animated them, philosophy would be impertinent, and history no better than an old almanack."—Lord Albert Conyngham was M.P. for Canterbury. Lord Spencer was a great breeder of prize cattle. Samuel Rogers, the poet, spent an enormous sum upon editions of his "Poems," and "Italy," illustrated by Turner and Stodhart. Unfortunately the paper, "hot pressed," after the fashion of the day, became freckled in a few years, and spoilt the engravings.—Mr. Young, originally a purser in a nobleman's yacht, was Lord Melbourne's very efficient Private Secretary.—The action brought by the Hon. Mr. Norton, a London Police magistrate, in 1836, against Lord Melbourne, was dismissed with costs, and Sir John Campbell's task, as counsel for the Premier, was an easy one. But people were getting tired of the dilettante ways of Lord Melbourne, of the bad finance of his colleagues, and of the bullying of O'Connell —the most formidable foe to England, in civil life, ever encountered by an English Ministry. Two years later, the Tories came in with a great majority. Praed died in July of this same year.

The intimate and even affectionate relations which existed between Lord Melbourne and the Queen, creditable as they were to both, was a not unnatural subject of jealousy to Tory politicians.—"A heavy blow and great discouragement to Protestantism in Ireland," was the phrase in which the Premier described his own proposals for the settlement of the tithe question in Ireland, July 1835, immediately after he assumed the Premiership a second time. The Lords accordingly rejected them.—Mr. Gibson Craig, M.P. for Edinburghshire (now called Midlothian), seconded the address on the meeting of the new Parliament in 1837. He stuck fast in his third sentence, and had to sit down. He did not rise again.—The concluding lines, a touching and spirited anticipation, which has by the event been so fully realized, form a fitting termination to this record of the fears and hopes and criticisms of half a century ago.]

King George the Third in Cockspur Street
Sits fast and firm upon his seat,
Though wickedly the rabble chat
About his coat and queue and hat,
Though boys, irreverently pert,
Bespatter him with mud and dirt,
And men of proper taste declare
The creature has no business there.
But we, my Lord, confess at last,
   Though you've your spiteful critics too,
That quite as firm and quite as fast
   Upon the Treasury Bench are you.

Opinions pass with years away;
   A doctrine is but for a season;
If loyalty's in vogue to-day,
   The rage to-morrow will be treason;
But whether Britain's favourite hue
Be pink or orange, red or blue,
We see your lordship still arrayed
In party's most triumphant shade;

And whether Fortune's smile or frown
Set Whig or Tory up or down,
We find your lordship's public views
Precisely what the Dame would choose.
What if in other times you fought
 For Church and State with Londonderry?
In all he said, in all he thought,
 Lord Melbourne's very like him—very!
What if, by Percival led on,
 You marched sedition's threats to stifle?
From Percival to dear Lord John
 The step is, after all, a trifle!
Canning, of course, was all divine,
But Shiel to-day is just as fine;
Vansittart's sums were neat and nice;
But Heaven! the ciphers of Spring Rice!
Though Mr. Hobhouse, as you know,
Was half a rebel long ago,
Sir John Cam Hobhouse now may be
A man with whom you quite agree;
And though 'tis certain Hume was once
Blockhead and blunderer, dolt and dunce,
Of late we may perhaps presume
There's something to be said for Hume!
Oh what a light will history shed
Hereafter round your lordship's head!
How consecrate to deathless fame
Your great forgetfulness of shame;

Of whom it must be gravely writ
    By pen of Whig and pen of Tory,
That after making praise of Pitt,
    And twining wreaths for Wellesley's glory,
You, that the State, through storm and calm,
    Might still have hands and heads to speed her,
Heard Evans brag without a qualm,
    And polled, without a blush for Leader!

Sure none should better know how sweet
The tenure of official seat,
Than one who every session buys
At such high rate the gaudy prize;
One who for this so long has borne
The scowl of universal scorn,
Has seen distrust in every look,
Has heard in every voice rebuke,
Has shrunk from Stanley's quick retort,
Has winced at Wakley's cool support;
Exulting yet—as home he goes
From sneering friends and pitying foes—
That shun him—loathe him—if they will,
He keeps the seals and salary still.

And truth to say, it must be pleasant
To be a minister at present;

To make believe to guide the realm
Without a hand upon the helm,
And wonder what with such a crew
A pilot e'er should find to do;
To hold what people are content
To fancy is the Government,
And touch extremely little of it
Except the credit and the profit;
To feel secure, when peril's near,
By shutting up the eye and ear;
To stop sedition's rude advances
By printing Normanby's romances;
To keep the Czar from mischief brewing
By never minding what he's doing;
To guard our colonies from harms
By slyly coaxing them to arms;
To share vacation's joyous hours
'Twixt Brighton's domes and Windsor's towers,
And gossip here, and gossip there,
With ladies dark, and ladies fair;
To sketch, when Fancy prompts exertion,
A note for Metternich's diversion,
Or protocol, so smoothly rounded
It must by twenty be expounded;
When Follett presses, Sugden poses,
To bid gay Stanley count the noses,
And leave the Cabinet's defence
To Bulwer's wit, and Blewitt's sense!

To hear demands for explanation
On India, Belgium, trade, taxation,
And answer, that perhaps they'll try
To give an answer by-and-by;
To save the Church and serve the Crown,
By letting others pull them down;
To promise, pause, prepare, postpone,
And end by leaving things alone;
In short, to earn the people's pay
By doing nothing every day—
These tasks, these joys, the Fates assign
To well-placed Whigs in 'thirty-nine.

We ascertain on looking back
In Plunket's tattered almanack—
Where, though we know there's nothing in it
To charm his lordship for a minute,
A student of more humble breeding
May find some scraps of curious reading—
That to the noble and the wise
The trust of England's destinies
Appeared, when George the Third was King,
To be a very serious thing.
Then statesmen found in State affairs
Laborious studies, anxious cares;
The joyless meal, the sleepless bed,
The aching heart, the plodding head;

Unheeded sacrifice of wealth,
Unpitied forfeiture of health;
Oft, tasked beyond its utmost strength,
The frail machine gave way at length,
And, fainting at his post of pride,
The nation's weary servant died.

But things are changed. The march of knowledge
Proceeds in Court as well as College.
The freshman on the banks of Cam,
Shall master, in a fortnight's cram,
Truths which, beside those waters muddy,
Cost great Sir Isaac years of study.
The lisping girl, who half conjectures
The meaning of a course of lectures,
Shall tell you tales of gas and steam,
Of which Lord Bacon did not dream.
What marvel, if the art to rule
Discoveries of the modern school
Have made so simple, as to fit
The compass of the largest wit?
What marvel, if on land and sea
Our destiny should guided be
With hardly half as much expense
Of time or trouble, thought or sense,
As Mr. Meynell may be able
To lavish yearly on his stable,

Lord Albert on his perfumed locks,
Lord Spencer on a Durham ox,
Sam Rogers on his beauteous books,
Or Holland on his corps of cooks?

While crowds expect him and abuse,
   Long hours, at his official quarters,
Patrons of negroes and of Jews,
   Whig pamphleteers and Church-rate martyrs.
While drowsy clerks at last despair,
   And Young begins to think of dining,
In lovely Sappho's elbow chair
   Behold our gay First Lord reclining.
Forgetful in his dreamy trance
   Which way the noisy world is going,
Of Turk or Russian, Spain or France,
   As little as his lackey knowing,
With his bright colleague he debates
   The Keepsake of the coming winter,
Admires the poems and the plates,
   Applauds the painter and the printer;
Lends, too, his judgment to revise
   Some startling tale or soothing sonnet,
Embellishes some "Scene of Sighs,"
   Or points some "Ode to Cynthia's bonnet;"
Yet now and then a respite asks
   From all the literary labour,

To share the sweet domestic tasks
　　Of her, his fair fantastic neighbour;
And turns from Mulgrave's dreary prose,
　　Or wakes from Morpeth's drowsy verses,
To measure baby's chin and nose,
　　And sip his caudle with the nurses.

Pity that Scandal should come by,
With pointing finger, squinting eye,
To hint reproach, to whisper harm,
To kindle doubt, to rouse alarm;
That such a course of faultless pleasure,
　　So very proper to engage
In his long listlessness of leisure
　　A Premier—of a certain age—
Should furnish food for jest and frown
To Themis in her wig and gown,
And entertain remotest climes,
Recorded in the *Globe* and *Times*.
Cruel to her, whose sullied fame
　　Scarce yet redeems its early whiteness!
Cruel to him, whose hearth became
　　Void, void of all that gave it brightness!
And cruel to the orphaned ones
　　Whose slumber often will recall
Those witching looks and winning tones!
　　Cruel, in short, to each and all

But plain John Campbell, who with ease
Bore off the verdict, and the fees.

Shift we the scene. More safely now
The Minister shall buzz and bow
In regions, where no comment rude
From lip or pen shall e'er intrude.
There he, the fond and favoured guest,
Shall look his liveliest, gloze his best,
On everything, or nothing, chatter,
And smoothly fawn, and softly flatter.
In curious tints shall he pourtray,
To make the royal listener gay,
Her pious Grandsire's stiff devotions,
Her moral Grandam's serious notions,
Her Uncle Frederic's bigot zeal,
Her Uncle William's wish for Peel.
Oft shall he whisper, deep and low,
The things he whispered long ago,
When in saloons he first began
To be a fascinating man,
'Ere yet the high ambition rose
To deal religion "heavy blows."
Oft shall he picture, with an air
Not very much the worse for wear,
How noble through the park she rides,
How graceful through the dance she glides,

How wonderful it is to see
Her fingers touch the ivory key;
And still, while Britain stands or falls
By dint of banquets and of balls,
While badinage directs the nation,
And politics are all flirtation,
Quick Ridicule shall smother half
Of her inexorable laugh;
Stern Censure, just prepared to preach,
Like Gibson Craig, shall lose her speech;
The Muse herself shall take upon her
The prudence of a Maid of Honour,
And, hushing her uncourtly spleen,
Sigh gently forth, "God save the Queen!"

That she may see, our Bright and Fair,
  How arduous is her path to fame,
How much of solemn thought and care
  An empire's interests fitly claim;
That she may know how poor 'twould seem
  In one who graces Britain's throne
To patronize a party's scheme
  Or make a favourite's cause her own;
That she may feel to Whom belong
  Alike the contest and the prize,
Whence springs the valour of the strong,
  Whence flows the counsel of the wise;

That she may keep in womanhood
   The heaven-born impulses of youth,
The zeal for universal good,
   The reverence for eternal Truth;
That she may seek the right and just;
   That she may shun the false and mean;
That she may win all love and trust,
   Blessing and blest—GOD SAVE THE QUEEN!

THE END.

www.ingramcontent.com/pod-product-compliance
Lightning Source LLC
Chambersburg PA
CBHW032352230426
43672CB00007B/674